D0778811

ANNA PAVLOVA

By Oleg Kerensky

BALLET SCENE

ANNA PAVLOVA

ANNA PAVLOVA

OLEG KERENSKY

E.P. Dutton & Co., Inc. / New York / 1973

LIKE *Ballet Scene*, this book is written in memory of my mother, who first took me to ballet and first talked to me about Anna Pavlova. It was my mother's childhood but vivid memory of Pavlova which helped me to understand her immense impact. In preparing this book I have found that my mother's gentleness, love of beauty, hatred of ugliness and cruelty, almost child-like innocence, and occasional fierce temper—all perhaps very Russian characteristics—provided a key to some aspects of Pavlova's somewhat similar personality. The world of ballet owes much of its present talent and popularity to Pavlova; I owe my small place in the world of ballet to my mother.

Contents

Photographs follow page 74

Introduction

by SIR FREDERICK ASHTON, C.H., C.B.E.

ANNA PAVLOVA, like all great theatrical geniuses, had a mysterious, enigmatic, undefinable quality. There has never been a dancer like her. In performance she was disturbing; even if you did not take to her, you could not help but be aware of the force, strength and charm of her personality, and of the utter absorption and genius of her interpretations, whatever role she was dancing.

It was not so much what she did—in many ways there was a certain sameness of steps—but how she did it. She transmuted the classical idiom to her personal demands, making it live. She was the most plastic dancer I have ever seen; every movement was felt through her entire body, through to the tips of her exquisite fingers, through to her large and luminous eyes. She could give life and individuality to the most trite of classical solos; she danced with a passionate abandon and intensity I have never seen equalled.

She also had consummate grace and an incredible bodily poise, possibly due to her unusually high-arched and expressive feet and the way her head and neck were set on her shoulders, which were used in a unique and personal way. She made much of her wonderful walk and she ran in a quite fantastic swift way. These great qualities were integral parts of her performances, as were her inimitable curtain calls. There was an element of melancholy and strangeness in her personality and she possessed to a very special extent the 'sens tragique', as well as a charming and delightful sense of comedy and style.

Her impact was felt throughout the world. Pavlova was the first dancer to become world famous; she thrilled and delighted audiences of every country from China to Peru, where I first saw her. There 'the immortal swan' injected a mere boy with her potent poison and he has never been the same since.

Preface

THERE is no doubt that Pavlova is the best-known dancer of all time. Nijinsky was a legend but his career was tragically short and he danced in comparatively few places. The great nineteenth-century romantic ballerinas are immortalized in prints but are known now only to specialist art-lovers and ballet enthusiasts. The great art critic and writer André Levinson thought Pavlova was greater than any of them: 'What we know about Camargo, Fanny Elssler, Grisi, Taglioni, does not suggest that any of them equalled Pavlova'. In our own time, Dame Margot Fonteyn and Rudolf Nureyev have become household names, and thanks to air travel, television and the cinema, they have been seen by a world-wide public. But the magic name 'Pavlova' is still the first to come to most people's lips if the conversation turns to ballet. Those who actually remember her can scarcely resist subjecting all other ballerinas or would-be ballerinas to unfavourable comparisons. 'Oh, but you should have seen Pavlova', is their irritating but often salutary response to excessive enthusiasm for the latest interpreter of *Giselle* or for the dancer rash enough to attempt Pavlova's most famous solo, generally known as *The Dying Swan*. Little girls who want to be ballerinas dream of becoming as famous as Pavlova, prizes are awarded in her name, and there is even a meringue and fruit gateau, which originated in Australia or New Zealand and which has recently become popular in England, called simply 'a Pavlova'. So Pavlova is immortalized as a dessert, just as Dame Nellie Melba, the Australian prima donna, is now best known for the ice-cream named after her.

Yet surprisingly little is known about Pavlova the dancer, and even less about Pavlova the woman. Her professional career lasted over thirty years and she performed in more towns all over the world than any other dancer, or indeed any other artist of any kind, before or since. A number of books have been written about her—by Victor Dandré (her husband), by two of her musical directors, and by various dancers who worked with her—and countless reminiscences and anecdotes have been published in magazines and broadcast on radio and television. Most of this material is laudatory, some of it exaggeratedly so. Most of those who danced in her company still retain an amazing devotion and loyalty to her memory; some of them simply are not willing to discuss any faults she may have had and indeed scarcely wish to acknowledge that she was a mere mortal. As one of them said to me: 'We worshipped her, and we don't want to discuss anything which could in any way spoil her image.' Or, as someone else put it, they talk about her 'as if she never even went to the toilet'. The most extreme devotion and loyalty comes from women; a few of the men in her company, by contrast, have written slighting and occasionally snide comments, mostly after they had been sacked or had failed to achieve the professional success they thought they deserved.

Reading these books and articles, I found a wealth of fascinating information, a conflict of opinions and even considerable disagreement over basic facts, which it has not been easy to disentangle. I did not find any single book which made me feel I knew Pavlova, or understood what made her 'tick'. I rapidly realized, however, that the image of her, fostered by some of her friends and by some of her dancers, as a kind of nun, is absurd. She could scarcely have been the magnetic and versatile dancer she was, excelling in coquettish and humorous roles as well as soulful and tragic ones, if she had not also lived a full life and taken an immense and lively interest in the world around her. It was not until I talked personally with a large number of her former dancers and colleagues, mostly in Britain and the United States, but also in Australia, that I gradually came to feel I understood the sort of woman she was and what gave her dancing its universal appeal. I also discovered that far from being a straightforward person, whose life-story might have been rather dull, she was in fact full of mystery. In this book, I have tried to present her as I dis-covered her; I hope that my admiration for her dancing and her personality shine clearly through its pages. But I have not attempted to conceal her blemishes, nor do I claim to have solved all the mysteries, some of which will probably remain forever.

In general I have indicated the sources of my information in the text, though not when the facts are well established and easily obtainable, when several people have given me the same information, or when my informants might be embarrassed by being named. I append lists of books which I have used: several of them are out of print and not readily available. I also append lists of dancers and others who worked for Pavlova with whom I have talked, and of others who supplied me with information and anecdotes, lent me cuttings, photographs and programmes, and guided me towards sources of information which I might otherwise have missed. I am extremely grateful to all of them, to others who offered or supplied material which I was not able to use, and to the friends who made my travels both practical and enjoyable by taking me into their homes: Mrs Helen Simpson in New York, Philip Guins in San Francisco, Don Cribb in Los Angeles, Allen McBride in Melbourne, and Richard Timmins and Roger Chree in Sydney. I am indebted to Richard Timmins too for his strong moral support during the writing of this book even though on this occasion it had to be given from the other side of the world.

I was helped with translation from the Russian, and guid-ance about Russian customs, by Mme Sophia Botcharsky and by my grandmother, Mrs O. L. Kerensky, and my father,

Dr O. A. Kerensky, and with translations from the German by Mrs Alan Blyth and Herr Peter Bremer. Once again I am indebted to Miss Patricia Entract, my friend and former colleague, for helping to collect and select the photos. The London Museum and the Dance Collection of the New York Library and Museum of the Performing Arts not only took the trouble to show me their collections of Pavlova photographs, and to make copies available, but also waived their publication fees. Miss Nadia Nerina and Messrs John O'Brien and David Leonard also generously gave me photos from their collections. Peter Hall, Joel Kasow and Roger Scales helped with checking the proofs. Finally I must thank Miss Josephine Rogers, my agent in New York, who prompted me to write the book.

I offer my apologies in advance to any helpers I have left unacknowledged. There have been so many that I fear I may not have done them all justice. Without them, this book could not have been written. Except when specifically stated, however, none of them can be held responsible for the accuracy of the facts or opinions included in it.

OLEG KERENSKY
December 1972

CHAPTER ONE

Russia

PERHAPS it is appropriate, in view of the mystery of her later private life, that even the circumstances of Pavlova's birth remain uncertain. She was born in St Petersburg (now Leningrad) and the date of her birth is variously given, in different books and articles, as 1881, 1882 and 1885. The earliest date seems to be correct; January 31st 1881 is the date of birth registered for her in the church book of a St Petersburg military hospital, and this fits in with the dates of her later career, making her ten years old (the normal age) when she entered the Imperial Ballet School in 1891. 1882 is the date given in Dandré's book, and it has been claimed that this date is given on a birth certificate in the Paget-Fredericks collection in California. But I have not been able to trace this certificate, and I doubt if it could be authentic. 1885 is a date that was probably calculated from some of Pavlova's own statements at a time when, like many other artists and many others of her sex, she did not wish to admit her true age.

Officially Pavlova's father was Matvey Pavlovitch Pavlov, a peasant and a reserve soldier—hence the birth registered in a military hospital. Pavlova never talked about her father and her face clouded if the subject was raised. If pressed, she would say she never knew her father, who died when she was two; this was a convenient way of avoiding further questions. She did not like to be addressed as Anna Matveyevna, which would have been the normal way for Russians to address her if her father was indeed Matvey. Instead Russian friends usually called her Anna Pavlovna, as if her father's Christian name had been Pavel. But this was a polite fiction; it was simply convenient for her to be 'Madame Pavlova' on formal occasions and 'Anna Pavlovna' to Russian friends. Non-Russian dancers called her simply 'Madame'; behind her back they referred to her, appropriately enigmatically, as 'X'. ('Pavlova' should be pronounced with the stress on the first syllable and a short 'o'; in other words it is pronounced 'Pávlov–a' not 'Pavlóeva'. The 'a' in 'Pavlov' is more like the 'a' in 'master' than the 'a' in 'apple'.)

It was often rumoured that Pavlova was illegitimate, and that her real father was a wealthy Jew. She herself confided to the American Russian-born impresario Sol Hurok that she was a Jewess, but she begged him not to reveal this till after her death. Presumably she shared a typical Russian prejudice of that period against Jews, and she of course presented herself to the world as a Russian artist, not a Jewish one. Being fairly conventional in her moral outlook, and living at the time she did, she would not have wanted the world to know she was illegitimate.

However a Russian friend of mine, Mme S. Botcharsky, told me that, years ago, she heard a Jewish friend called Vladimir Poliakoff say that he was Pavlova's half-brother. There was no reason for him to invent such a story. He came of a wealthy Jewish banking family, who were well-known as patrons of the arts. His father was Lazar Jacovlevitch Poliakoff, who held the hereditary rank of 'dvoranin' ('gentleman') which was rare among Jews. Lazar's brother Samuel helped to finance the training of several eminent violinists, including Kreisler, Heifetz and Elman.

If Lazar Poliakoff was Pavlova's father, as it seems reasonable to assume, Pavlova's belief that her special talent was inherited becomes more explicable. The Poliakoffs originally came from a dancing sect in Georgia. Another celebrated dancer, Ida Rubinstein, was also a member of the family. It is a fascinating thought that Pavlova and Rubinstein were probably relations by marriage, though not by blood. Two other Poliakoffs have made theatrical careers in England.

The actress Vera Lindsay, who was well known on the London stage in the 1930s and who was later married to Sir Gerald Barry and to the art critic John Russell, was born Vera Poliakova and was Lazar Poliakoff's granddaughter. So she may have been Pavlova's half-niece. (She never heard her father speak of any relationship with Pavlova, but such things would not have been discussed in her rather Victorian family; on reflection, she thinks that the relationship is perfectly possible, as her grandfather married quite late.) The young writer Stephen Poliakoff, who had a play produced at the Royal Court Theatre in London in 1972, when he was only 19, is also a distant relation.

The mixture of Jewish and Russian blood, and the knowledge that she was illegitimate, help to explain a great deal about Pavlova's personality and even about her dancing. Levinson said she brought Russian lyrical inspiration and Jewish ardour to the great classic ballets. 'This propitious mixing of races was at the origin of her genius. There was almost something oriental in her. This mixture of bloods explains the universality of her art.' It also explains why Pavlova had a sensitivity of personality and a refinement of appearance which one would not expect to have found in the daughter of a peasant soldier. She looked much more like a Jewish girl of good family than like a Russian working-class or peasant girl.

Pavlova's mother, the wife of the soldier Matvey Pavlov, was poor and is generally described as a laundrywoman. She may have been slightly superior to that; Mme Manya Charchevnikova, who was Pavlova's costume-maker and friend for many years and who knew the family in Russia, says that Pavlova's mother was at one time in charge of the linen at the Imperial Ballet School and later ran a laundry shop of her own in St Petersburg. But she was definitely not an educated woman, and could not write very well. Her name was Lyubov Fedorovna Pavlova, she came from a village near Tver (now Kalinin) and she was thirty-three when Pavlova was born. A document still kept in the

theatre archives in Leningrad describes her as being married
to a soldier but refers to Anna Pavlova as her daughter by her
first marriage, with no indication who this first husband was.

Like all Russian peasant and working women, Lyubov
Pavlova was a devout Christian and it was as a Russian
Orthodox Christian, not as a Jew, that Anna was brought up.
As in most Russian homes, there was an ikon in the living-
room and the young Pavlova got into the habit of telling
the picture of the Virgin Mary about her childish hopes and
fears. She also formed the habit of crossing herself regularly
in the Russian Orthodox way, as she continued to do all her
life; she always crossed herself before going on to the stage.
Her mother, though poor, regularly provided a Christmas
tree with candles and golden fruit, and an Easter egg containing toys; in later years, Pavlova attached great importance to Christian seasonal festivities and made a point of
parties, complete with presents and Christmas tree or
Easter eggs, for her dancers.

Pavlova was a delicate child. She was born two months
premature on January 31st and she was so tiny and weak
that the neighbours thought she would not survive. She
was baptized without delay, on February 3rd. This was St
Anna's day in the Russian Orthodox Church calendar,
hence her Christian name. Anna spent many of her first
months wrapped in cotton wool and in childhood she
succumbed to various illnesses, including diphtheria and
scarlet fever, which were more serious then than they are
now. At the age of four she upset a samovar, containing
boiling water for making tea, and scalded her left hand so
badly that it was scarred for life.

Because of her poor health, the young Pavlova spent a
great deal of time at a *dacha* (villa) at Ligovo, a summer
resort just outside St Petersburg. (According to Dandré,
this dacha belonged to her grandmother, but when I asked
Mme Manya about this, she said that Pavlova never spoke
of a grandmother, but of an aunt. There is no mention of
either aunt or grandmother in Pavlova's own brief auto-

biographical sketch. Indeed she wrote that she remembered her mother's furniture being moved to the *dacha*, which suggests that it was rented for them by someone, rather than belonging to a relation. I cannot help wondering if the *dacha* was contributed by Pavlova's father, as it seems unlikely that any of her mother's relations would have owned such a place.)

Like many Russians, Pavlova developed a deep love for her native countryside, for which she pined through all her years abroad, preferring the simple landscapes of northern Russia, which she found 'understandable', to more exotic scenery. She liked collecting flowers, especially snowdrops and lilies of the valley, and berries and mushrooms. It was at Ligovo that she developed her great feeling for nature, which remained with her always and inspired several of her most famous dances. She also had some lessons in sculpture there, and in Russian grammar and literature.

Pavlova recounted that her first introduction to ballet was at the age of eight, when her mother took her to *The Sleeping Beauty* as a Christmas treat. (This must have been in January 1890, when *The Sleeping Beauty* was created and when Pavlova was almost nine.) Her mother sensibly prepared her for the ballet by telling her the story in advance, and saying 'You are going to enter fairyland'. Pavlova got very excited and could not withhold a shout of delight when the curtain rose. Afterwards her mother asked her if she would like to dance something like the waltz; Pavlova's answer showed that the visit had been more successful than her mother had bargained for. 'I should rather dance the part of the Princess', she said. 'One day I shall be the Princess and shall dance upon the stage of this theatre.'

Nor was this just a passing notion. The young Pavlova insisted on dancing lessons, despite her mother's pointing out that a career as a dancer would mean leaving home and virtually living at the Ballet School. 'I have no wish to leave you, Mama dear,' Pavlova quoted herself as saying, 'but if it's necessary for me to part with you in order to become a ballerina, I shall have to resign myself to it.' After days of tears her mother was cajoled into taking her to see the director of the ballet school, who told the determined little eight-year-old to come back when she was ten.

For nearly two years, Pavlova spent more time in the country, exploring the woods and cloister-like alleys made by the fir trees, admiring the butterflies, weaving wreaths of wild flowers, and imagining herself to be the Sleeping Beauty in the enchanted castle. Later she sometimes said that the first tragedy of her life was when she was dancing with the butterflies and a boy came and caught one, crushing it to death. She felt 'as if some giant had reached up his hand and pulled down the sky'—a reaction remarkably similar to Swanilda's dismay, in the first act of the ballet *Coppélia*, when her boy friend Franz does the same thing. The young girl read Krylov's fables (partly based on La Fontaine's but with a very Russian character and social relevance) aloud to her mother, who also taught her to sew.

But Pavlova never forgot her desire to be a dancer. When she was ten, she reminded her mother that it was time to try the ballet school again. This time she was examined, for health, intelligence and gracefulness, to see if she met the rigorous standards required for training by the Imperial Ballet. First she had to stand still, walk and run, then to submit to a thorough physical and medical examination. There were also tests in singing scales, writing, reading and arithmetic. Competition for the available places was very keen, as not only was it a great honour to be in the Imperial Ballet School but it also meant completely free education, including board, lodging and clothes, all provided by the state. About a third of the candidates were usually accepted; Pavlova was of course one of the successful ones.

Later she recalled that she and her mother both wept when she left for the school. 'I was relinquishing the happy peaceful life of home, under the protection of the silver Virgin, and entering the very trying, intoxicating life of a

widely different world, the word of art and of the stage. My
mother realized that there could be no turning back and
that was why she felt sad; for although one may fail to find
happiness in theatrical life, one never wishes to give it up
after having once tasted its fruits.' Whether or not Pavlova
and her mother really had these prophetic thoughts at the
time, it certainly must have been a big wrench for a ten-
year-old girl to move from the sheltered position of an only
child at home to the disciplined and competitive life of a
boarding school.

Here is Pavlova's own description: 'To enter the School
of the Imperial Ballet is to enter a convent where frivolity
is banned, and where merciless discipline reigns. Every
morning at eight, the solemn tolling of a big bell would
put an end to our sleep. We dressed under the stern eye of
a governess, whose duty it was to see that all hands were
kept perfectly clean, all nails in good trim, and all teeth
carefully washed. When we were ready, we went to prayers
which were sung by one of the older pupils in front of an
ikon under which a tiny flickering lamp was burning like a
little red star. At nine, breakfast—tea, bread and butter—
was served, and immediately afterwards the dancing lessons
began.'

For the next eight years, Pavlova progressed up the school,
dancing in studios decorated with portraits of the Tsars,
going for walks in crocodile round and round the school
garden, never being allowed to talk to the boy pupils, and
sleeping in a large dormitory with a governess screened off
at one end and five senior girls in a recess at the other end.
She learnt fencing and music, as well as dancing, and of
course ordinary academic subjects. Her mother visited her
every Sunday and Pavlova spent the holidays at home. The
most exciting days at the school were when the Tsar called
to inspect, or to attend a student performance. Once
Pavlova burst into tears because Tsar Alexander embraced
another little girl—'I want the Emperor to kiss *me*', she
cried. The Tsar and members of the royal family sometimes

took tea quite informally in the school dining-room. 'We were not in the least embarrassed by their presence', Pavlova said. 'The Emperor and Empress were so kind, so very much like a father and mother, that we were quite at ease with them.'

Other excitements were provided by the chance to appear from time to time, as students, in the ballet performances at the Maryinsky Theatre, particularly in the last-act divertissements of the big spectacular classics. Rehearsals for these performances were a welcome interruption to the afternoon academic classes (dance and music classes were in the mornings), and the students were usually taken to the theatre in large four-wheeled carriages, in which they would be accompanied by a governess, a maid and a beadle. Their favourite ballet was *Paquita*, because the children of the school took part in the smartly-dressed Polish mazurka, which was always encored.

The school uniform was old-fashioned, even for those days: a blue serge dress with a low-cut tight bodice and a full gathered skirt down to the instep, worn with a black or white alpaca apron, white stockings and black pumps. The colours of the uniform varied according to seniority and rigid distinctions were kept between the older and younger girls. It was an artificial and cloistered life, entirely dedicated to the ballet, and may explain the charm and spirituality of the great Russian ballerinas of that time, which have not been equalled since.

The technical training for classical ballet is arduous and demanding. It is not just a matter of learning to dance on the points of the feet, but of turning out the legs from the hips, of jumping lightly and balancing correctly, of developing a harmonious line of the arms and legs, of looking graceful when held in the arms of a partner, and of learning a whole series of steps. The pupils of the Imperial Ballet School were also taught national folk-dances and historical dances and they learnt about the history of ballet and the art of make-up.

One of Pavlova's first teachers was the former ballerina Ekaterina Vazem, who feared that the young girl would not be strong enough to make a ballerina. But Pavlova's special gifts were spotted from the beginning by a veteran male dancer, Pavel Gerdt, who specialized in characterization, make-up, nobility and elegance; his pupils were famous for their soft arms, for their expressiveness, and their beauty of line. Gerdt was also an exceptionally considerate and helpful partner. He tried to save the delicate Pavlova from over-work and from attempting too many difficult technical feats. He used to tell her that technique would come in time, but that she had a natural grace which could never be acquired; he revived some old romantic ballets specially for her. Similarly, the great Swedish teacher Christian Johansson forgave Pavlova's lack of good natural 'turn-out', because of her poetic qualities and beautiful line.

In her final year at school, Pavlova was also taught by the famous Italian ballet-master Enrico Cecchetti, who was to be her private teacher and friend later in her career. But he was mainly interested in difficult feats of virtuosity, which were too hard for Pavlova when she was a student.

Tamara Karsavina, four years younger than Pavlova and destined to become almost as famous a ballerina, recalled that Pavlova seemed weaker than the other students and was given cod-liver oil to feed her up. Her dancing style also seemed gentler and more ethereal than was usual at a time when the strong Italian ballerina Pierina Legnani was all the rage and Russian dancers were competing to imitate her thirty-two *fouettés* (spins on one foot) in *Swan Lake*.

Nevertheless Pavlova's special talent was apparent, not only to Gerdt and Johansson but also to her contemporary Michel Fokine, who later became Diaghilev's great revolutionary choreographer and the creator of Pavlova's most famous solo. He danced with Pavlova regularly in those early years and staged a special school production of a shortened version of *La Fille Mal Gardée* for her. In Pavlova's last year at the school the great classical choreographer

Marius Petipa revived *The Two Stars* and allowed her to dance one of the stars with Fokine as Adonis. She was very successful in both these ballets and it was widely realized that she had an unusual lyrical gift. Gerdt arranged an old-fashioned ballet about nymphs and dryads for her graduation performance in 1899 at the Mikhailovsky Theatre. She was taken into the Imperial Ballet, not as a mere member of the corps de ballet but as one of the coryphées, the girls who danced together in groups of three or four. This was an unusual honour.

Pavlova's natural aptitude for the stage was clearly demonstrated at her first public appearance at the Maryinsky Theatre; she tripped over the prompter's box while doing some pirouettes and fell with a bump with her back to the audience. Undaunted, she turned to smile and curtsy, as if the fall was natural and even planned. (Three years later, when she fell intentionally while dancing the 'Bacchanale' in *The Seasons*, her fall was so realistic that her mother, sitting in the top gallery, burst into tears and rushed backstage to attend her daughter!) Her promise was immediately perceived by the distinguished critic Valerian Svetlov, who first saw her at her graduation performance, in the ballet about nymphs and dryads. 'Slender and graceful, vibrating like a reed,' he wrote in his book *Terpsichore*, 'with the face of an innocent Spanish girl, light as a feather and ethereal, she looked like a fragile Sèvres statuette. From time to time in her poses and attitudes one could see something classical and if at that moment she had worn some drapery she would have looked like a Tanagra figurine. With a childish innocence she acted a coquettish scene with a young peasant and with playful frolics she danced with imaginary wood nymphs. Everything about her was so youthfully gay and charming that one could not say more about her dancing except that her face was so expressive that one felt that the acting was all her own and not something learnt or drilled into her by the school. In a separate variation from Drigo's *Vestal Virgin* one could feel something even bigger, something that, without imagining oneself to be a prophet, made one foresee in this fragile dancer a future great artist. I do not know how many marks were awarded to her by the expert jury, but I gave her the highest mark, 12. Afterwards, finding myself out in the cold rain and remembering this young wood nymph, I added a plus to the mark.'

'After that', Svetlov continued, 'I left St Petersburg and lost sight of the young wood nymph. Late in the autumn, as soon as the ballet season began, I saw her again. By that time she was already on the main stage. The pupil Pavlova was already Madame Pavlova II [there was an older dancer called Pavlova, who was no relation]. She was as fragile and graceful as before, but one could see in her sad eyes suspense, maybe a silent question about her future.' If there was a silent question, Pavlova seems to have been fairly confident about the answer. As at the age of eight, she was still determined to be, not just a good dancer, but a prima ballerina. After one of her first solo appearances she told an admirer that she would become world-famous or disappear entirely. She was a perfectionist and by no means content to relax and enjoy her early success. Once she spent her holidays in Milan studying with the ballerina Beretta to strengthen her technique. In Russia she took private lessons with Eugenia Sokolova, a very conservative and old-fashioned teacher, whom Pavlova adored. Sokolova had a remarkable knowledge of the steps and style required for the older ballets, and played a crucial role in helping Pavlova to bring those ballets back to life. She also taught her the importance of carefully-rehearsed curtain-calls; she insisted that the dancer should never simply walk on flat feet to acknowledge the applause but should give a 'performance', tripping lightly towards the curtain, curtsying to the boxes on each side, then to the centre, then to the stalls, and finally looking up to smile before curtseying to the gallery. In later years many people found Pavlova's curtain-calls almost as exciting as her actual dancing.

After Sokolova, in 1905 Pavlova started taking private

lessons with Cecchetti, eventually persuading him to close his private school and devote himself exclusively to her for about two years. He gave her exercises to strengthen her back and her confidence. Some people even began to worry that her dancing might get too 'Italian', too technical, and lose its natural softness and charm. They need not have worried; Pavlova continued to go from strength to strength. She had become a 'second soloist' in 1902 and a 'first soloist' a year later. In 1905 she was officially appointed a 'ballerina', and in 1906 she became a 'prima ballerina'. This quick promotion was all the more remarkable when it is remembered that many of the young dancers had influential relatives who had been famous dancers themselves. But Pavlova's dancing and personality were so unusual, and so attractive, that she quickly gained the admiration of balletomanes. One of the first to succumb was the veteran General Bezobrazov, who wrote in a St Petersburg newspaper: 'This artist reminds us, by the style of her performance, of some long-past romantic days.'

Pavlova was lucky to start her career at a time when the management of the Maryinsky Theatre was prepared to break traditional rules and to give young dancers more opportunities than they had had previously. She danced Zulme, one of the two leading wilis in *Giselle*, in her very first season; everyone watched *her* and General Bezobrazov said 'she looks like Taglioni'. She also danced the secondary role of Aurora in a now-forgotten Drigo-Petipa ballet, *The Awakening of Flora*. By her second season she was dancing the title-role of Flora. Svetlov noted that her talent was quickly blossoming and gathering strength. Her mime was strong, her movement expressive and her dancing extraordinarily light. By her third season she had so many admirers that they formed a definite group, known as 'Pavlovtzi', followers of Pavlova. And then she danced the title-role in *Giselle*, although she was not yet officially a 'ballerina'.

The Awakening of Flora was a light-hearted curtain-raiser, usually cast with young dancers. Pavlova stood out for her high, long aerial jumps, and the softness and delicacy of her movements. Nevertheless Svetlov qualified his praise with the remarks that Pavlova was not yet fully equal to all the technical demands of the choreography and was also very nervous. *Giselle* was a much bigger and more important success. Nowadays it is regarded as one of the most difficult and rewarding ballerina roles, and it is often described as the 'Hamlet of the dance'. But at that time it was not very popular; even Svetlov described it as a minor ballet! Indeed it was Pavlova, with her skill in the old-fashioned romantic style, who brought *Giselle* back into favour, first in Russia and later all over the world.

Reviewing her first *Giselle*, Svetlov noted subtle nuances in her dancing and poetic feeling in her whole interpretation. Her romantic period style was maintained consistently throughout the ballet. But the mime 'did not entirely satisfy the spectators, not because she did not act well, but because in her acting one could see many quite different intentions, which did not blend into one artistically whole image'. Her second act was evidently more successful than her first; Svetlov said it would be difficult to find a more suitable dancer, and he constantly reiterated her lightness and softness.

In the autumn of the same year Pavlova danced her second *Giselle* and the improvement was dramatic. By this time Svetlov thought Pavlova was in complete command of the role, no longer tentative or nervous but strong and self-possessed. She was touching, graceful and extremely stylish. 'This style, this "cachet" of olden times, was imprinted on her interpretation,' he wrote. 'I do not speak about her external appearance: a clever actress can easily achieve with a suitable dress and coiffure the correct external style. But only a great artist could immerse herself in the very heart of old times and bring them back to life for us. And I do not hesitate to say that Pavlova is a great artist who has an inborn natural artistic sensitivity and a very strong individuality ... If anyone wishes to have an absolutely exceptional and priceless artistic experience, they *must* see Pavlova in *Giselle*.'

Levinson particularly admired Pavlova's interpretation of Giselle's mad scene because it was *danced*. He said that most Russian ballerinas of that period did a realistic mimed imitation of madness which was not in keeping with the stylized conventions of this ballet. But Pavlova repeated the light-hearted dances of the earlier part of the ballet, doing them in a broken, mechanical way as if fragments of memories were jumbled in her mind. She danced hesitantly and slowly, as if listening to a far-away voice. (Both ways of doing the mad scene are still seen today, and Pavlova's way always strikes me as both more moving and more appropriately romantic.)

Another of Pavlova's big successes during the 1902–3 season was in the leading role of *Bayaderka*, one act of which is nowadays performed in the west under the title *La Bayadère*. Svetlov found it even more successful than her *Giselle*. *Bayaderka* was a revival of a ballet which Petipa had originally created in 1877; the ballerina role of Nikiya was considered more difficult and more important than Giselle, and it was also Petipa's favourite of his own creations. He hurt the feelings of many more senior dancers by selecting the young Pavlova, who was still not officially a ballerina, to dance it.

Svetlov noted wryly that at first the critics were a bit uncertain and reserved, 'as they always are when reviewing a newcomer in a difficult role'. He himself had no doubts, and the other critics soon came to recognize Pavlova's special talent. Svetlov wrote of her tragic mime, making the drama eloquent, her beautiful poses, like statues, and the lightness and quality of her dancing. He particularly admired her in the death-scene: Nikiya is killed by the bite of a snake hidden in a basket of flowers, and then her soul dances, bathed in moonlight, in the vale of death. This scene had poetic mysticism and lyric charm, and involved a great deal of technical virtuosity. Svetlov said:

'To write about *Bayaderka* is to write about Pavlova; all the rest remains in the background and colourless. When this young, beautiful and graceful ballerina appears on the stage one feels exalted, seeing her sincerity and her simple charm. Not for a second does one doubt her love for Solor, her hate for the Brahmin, her tragic grief when the man she loves betrays her, and her great suffering before she dies. Her face marvellously reflects all her feelings. The role does not possess her. She is in full possession and control of the role. Pavlova's talent for mime has elements of a real tragic artist. She has another precious gift: her creations are entirely individual. This ballerina never imitates or presents copies; she creates in a hypnotic state which possesses her while she is in the role. I am writing so much about her talent as a mime because I really love it. One sees it very rarely in the ballet world.' Svetlov commented that Pavlova's journey to Milan to study with Beretta might not have been strictly necessary, but her pirouettes had become more precise and her dancing on the points of her feet more assured. And he added: 'It is a long time since the Maryinsky Theatre has heard such a stormy ovation as the one received by Pavlova after her first performance of *Bayaderka*.'

It was soon generally agreed that Pavlova brought more dramatic impact to *Bayaderka* than any previous ballerina had done. The story was, after all, corny and conventional and not really to be taken seriously. It was set in India and concerned the rivalry of a princess and a temple-dancer (or 'bayadère') for Solor, a handsome warrior; the princess orders a snake to be hidden to poison the temple-dancer. After her death, the warrior dreams of her spirit, then forgets her again to marry the princess, only to have his wedding celebrations interrupted and destroyed by divine vengeance. (This was the original version of the ballet, which Pavlova performed. In Soviet productions the ballet ends with Solor's vision of the dead bayadère in the Kingdom of Shades—the scene which is now presented on its own by various companies in the west.)

Levinson said that this conventional story and setting were rejuvenated and made good by Pavlova's deep and delicate humanity. 'The oriental and melodramatic tinsel and dross suddenly shone with all the gold of the spirit.' He gave an example of what he called theatrical auto-suggestion. 'The spirit of the bayadère is born entirely under the eyes of the spectators. In a silent love duet with the warrior, the earthly soul of the bayadère flies out and bursts into flame in a series of excited gestures and looks; then she bends and writhes under the whip of insult, runs sadly up against some invisible barrier, like a moth against a window-pane. Her weak shoulders (magnificent in anger and scorn) and her thin arms meekly carry the burden of overwhelmingly conquered feelings. Admittedly, Pavlova does not give any detailed or accurate imitation of native behaviour. But, all the time, an imperceptible breath of exoticism emanates from her being. It is like the aroma of certain eastern perfumes which penetrates, if the poets are to be believed, through the crystal sides of the bottle.'

After further detailed description of Pavlova's acting as the betrayed temple-dancer, Levinson went on to contrast this with her ethereal appearance in the land of the spirits, in the 'white' act of the ballet. 'All psychological interpretation disappears; the impossible love, stronger than death, which evaporated in the mimed scene, is reborn in pure classical dance. Thus the symbolic meaning of the ballet, hidden by the childish and pretty external trappings, becomes clear. From the moment that Pavlova touches it, everything in this most ephemeral of the arts becomes symbolic.'

Other full-length classics which Pavlova danced in the early years of her career included *Paquita*, *Le Corsaire*, *La Fille Mal Gardée* and *Don Quixote*. In addition Petipa staged many smaller works for her, notably a revival of an old French ballet, *Ondine*, known in Russia as *The Nayad and the Fisherman*, to music by Pugni. Svetlov thought this ballet too old-fashioned and the music too trivial for audiences 'spoilt by Tchaikowsky and Glazunov'. Nor did he think the dances choreographed for Pavlova suited her style. 'The most important and charming aspect of her performance was her full understanding of the role. The more one sees of this ballerina the greater is one's conviction that her miming ability is one of the most characteristic sides of her talent.' There was a scene by a well in which Pavlova appeared as a boy. 'It was just right for her slender, supple figure and is such a beautiful picture that, once seen, it can never be forgotten.'

Pavlova was less happy in ballets that relied entirely on technical virtuosity, rather than on drama and interpretation. Svetlov said that when she first danced in *Paquita* she found it difficult to cope with what was virtually a music-hall divertissement, a Spanish fiesta seen through conventional theatrical eyes. But she succeeded in giving the dances a new look full of original beauty. Her solos in the style of a bolero stunned the public by their grace and suppleness. No other ballerina brought Spanish dances such elegance, lightness and *éclat*. She bubbled with temperament and passion, took up sculptural poses, always showed a beautiful 'line', and delighted in the nimble, intricate, quick footwork. She was also extremely dramatic when opportunity offered, as in the mime scene in an inn. It was *Paquita* which led a critic to write: 'Her dancing is like the flying sound which comes from a harp.' Like all Pavlova's roles, it carried her original and personal stamp, and indeed Petipa created a special solo for her in which she appeared to defy the law of gravity and flutter like a bird in the air. Svetlov noted some technical deficiencies: her pirouettes were not quite precise and in the *Grand Pas* she made some mistakes. 'But these details were not important. What was important was the enchantment. She is a poet of choreography, a poet by the grace of God.'

The role of Medora in the ballet *Le Corsaire* gave her more dramatic opportunities. Svetlov believed that Byron must have imagined just such a Greek girl when he wrote the poem on which the ballet was based. The dances suited her

—light and graceful with just the right amount of virtuosity —and she accomplished them without any apparent effort. She played the slightly daring grotto scene, which was previously acted with crude realism, with subtle and elegant nuances. In the pas de deux her *renversés* followed by an *attitude* when she fell on her knees, struck Svetlov as a marvel. Her *fouettés en diagonale* were 'much more elegant than simple *fouettés*'. And she did some superb cabrioles in an extra scene, with music by Debussy, which was specially added to a ballet whose main score was already a mixture of Adam and Pugni.

It was in 1905, when she officially became a 'ballerina', that Pavlova first danced the principal role of Kitry in the ballet *Don Quixote*. This role involves no mime and Pavlova abandoned herself entirely to the dance, using all her charm and grace. Her dancing had such beauty that the technical effects were scarcely noticed. The exacting St Petersburg audience was very impressed. Levinson was struck by the way she adopted Spanish gestures and movements, while preserving an idealized and classical style. At this moment he felt she embodied the future of the Russian tradition and the national ballet.

It must not be imagined that all this praise heaped upon Pavlova meant that she was the only star in the Russian balletic firmament. On the contrary, this was the period when the Imperial Russian Ballet was richest in great ballerinas, many of them world-famous. Names like Kshessinskaya, Trefilova, Egorova, Geltzer, Kyasht and Karsavina are known to everyone who has read the history of ballet, and most of them became famous and distinguished teachers in the west after they left Russia. Each of them had her specialities: either exceptionally strong technique, or humour, or a dignified classical style, or lyricism, or dramatic skill. None of them, except possibly Karsavina, was as versatile as Pavlova and none of them, again except for Karsavina, attached such importance to the interpretation of a role and the creation of a mood. Not that Pavlova was above revelling in dance for its own sake, any more than she minded conventional music or easy effects to excite an audience. Her very first appearance with Nijinsky, in 1906, was in a pas de huit inserted in the opera *Don Giovanni*, in which she replaced Trefilova.

Fokine recalled that in his early days of dancing with Pavlova they were simply anxious to show off whatever they could do best. She did pirouettes with Fokine giving her a push to help her around, and he displayed his elevation, disregarding musical phrases and accents. Pavlova would say 'Take it easy, we've got plenty of time', or 'Hurry, hurry'. The experienced ballet conductor, Riccardo Drigo, who wrote so much 'hack' ballet music, would linger over a tremolo while Pavlova found and held her balance and he would watch to launch the drumbeat when she froze into her final pose. Fokine used to tell Pavlova that this circus-like technique was not artistic. But she would reply that the audience liked it, and without an effective ending to a dance they would not have any success. Fokine also complained about the conventional mime gestures in which he would declare 'I love you', Pavlova would reply 'No, you will desert me', 'Never', 'Swear it'—an exchange which was identical in virtually every classical ballet, whether it was *Bayaderka*, *Paquita*, *Coppélia* or *Giselle*. At that period the ballerina was simply herself on the stage, wearing her own hair-style, acknowledging her friends in the boxes with a smile, and inserting her favourite steps into every ballet. When Fokine partnered Pavlova in this kind of dance, he believed in it while it was happening. 'It seemed important and good, especially when it went well. But after performances I would ask myself: "Is all this necessary? What does it mean?" ' At first Fokine's doubts did not worry Pavlova but gradually he persuaded her that a ballerina should subordinate herself to a role and should become just one of the elements, even if the most important one, in a coherent production. 'Pavlova responded to my ideas wholeheartedly, with inspiration', he said later.

The collaboration between Fokine and Pavlova started with *La Vigne* (*The Vineyard*) created by Fokine at the request of the members of the ballet company. It was the first ballet he made for them, as distinct from works for the students of the school, and was staged at a charity performance in 1906 in aid of a new school for poor children in the village of Greblovo, just outside St Petersburg. (Pavlova also led a processional dance at this performance.) The music was by Anton Rubinstein and the story was about a group of drinking companions in a rich man's cellar. Fokine appeared as the host and Pavlova, as one of the wines, danced a pas de deux with him; other famous ballerinas, including Karsavina and Lydia Kyasht, also took part.

The following year Pavlova danced in two more Fokine ballets at another charity performance. (It was organized by Victor Dandré, and Fokine in his memoirs says it was in aid of the Society for the Prevention of Cruelty to Children. Other sources, including the appendix to Fokine's memoirs, state that it was again in aid of the Greblovsky School.) One was *Eunice*, a two-act work with a story based on the novel *Quo Vadis* and with conventional ballet music, which Fokine did not like, by Shtcherbashev. It was an experiment in recreating the world of antiquity, and Fokine excluded the usual ballet steps, developing a plastic style influenced by Isadora Duncan, who had recently appeared in St Petersburg. Fokine wanted it to be a barefoot ballet, but this was forbidden at the Imperial Theatres, so toes, complete with coloured toe-nails, as well as heels and knees were painted on the dancers' tights! Pavlova appeared as a slave girl and did a dance of the seven veils. Fokine claimed he distributed the veils in such a way that Pavlova did not appear bulky, and at the removal of each veil the audience's attention was focussed on a different part of her body. The leading role of Eunice was taken by Kshessinskaya who had to dance between eight sharp swords sticking out of the ground. After the first night, Pavlova took over the leading part, and Karsavina took over Pavlova's. Karsavina says that

Pavlova looked like a figure out of a Pompeian frieze and infused a definite sense of style into the ballet. She was consistent and exquisite.

At the same charity performance, Fokine also produced his first version of *Chopiniana*, the ballet which in a revised form eventually became world-famous as *Les Sylphides*. In its original form it was a very different ballet from the one we now know; it began with the ensemble doing Polish ballroom dances and then it went on to show Chopin sitting at the piano, suffering from hallucinations. Then there were other national dances. The music consisted of various Chopin piano pieces, orchestrated by Glazunov. Most of these pieces already existed, but Fokine persuaded Glazunov to orchestrate the Waltz in C Sharp Minor specially for the ballet, because he wanted a romantic number, in a long white Taglioni skirt, as a contrast with the national dances. It was this waltz which was danced by Pavlova, with Mikhail Oboukhov. It was retained as the pas de deux in Fokine's later versions of the ballet, and is still danced by the leading ballerina in *Les Sylphides*.

Fokine wrote that in composing this waltz he was not trying to win applause, nor to satisfy the ballerina; he could not conceive of any spectacular stunts to such poetic, lyrical music, so there were no flashy show-off steps, as in most pas de deux at that time. He added: 'Pavlova and Oboukhov marvellously executed the composition, changing nothing, adding nothing, omitting not the slightest detail. I began to see the realization of my dreams, my hopes, for a ballet totally different from what I was accustomed to seeing at the Maryinsky Theatre.' He also said: 'Had Pavlova not performed so marvellously, so delightfully, the Chopin waltz, I might never have created *Les Sylphides*.'

When Fokine revived *Chopiniana* a year later, it became a whole series of romantic dances in the Taglioni style, the first version of *Les Sylphides*. This time Pavlova danced the mazurka and it was Karsavina who danced the waltz—with Nijinsky. Fokine wrote: 'Pavlova flew across the entire stage during the mazurka. If one measured this flight in terms of inches, it actually would not be particularly high; many other dancers jump higher. But Pavlova's position in mid-air, her slim body—in short, her talent—consisted in her ability to create the impression not of jumping but of flying through the air. Pavlova had mastered the difference between jumping and soaring, which is something that cannot be taught.'

Fokine also commented wryly that in later years various ballerinas tried to distinguish themselves in this ballet by wearing different coloured wreaths on their heads. 'Pavlova also distinguished herself from the rest, but not by the colour of her wreath. She was an ardent devotee of my reforms and continuously asked whether her chaplet were placed correctly and if her hair style looked right.'

Between the two versions of *Chopiniana*, Fokine created the solo for which Pavlova is best known and with which she will always be associated, the solo which became famous all over the world as *The Dying Swan*. (In his memoirs Fokine says it was created in 1905, but this appears to have been a slip of memory, as Soviet authorities say it was definitely in 1907 at a charity concert in aid of destitute and unmarried mothers). Pavlova went to Fokine and told him she had been asked to dance at a concert being given by the opera chorus in the Hall of Nobles. She asked Fokine to suggest some music. It so happened that he had been practising Saint-Saens' piece, *The Swan*, on the mandoline. He sensed that the thin, fragile Pavlova would be well-cast as a swan and so he suggested this music; Pavlova immediately agreed. Fokine composed the dance in a few minutes—it was almost an improvisation. He danced in front, or alongside her, demonstrating how to curve the arms and suggesting various poses. The dance was fairly simple technically; it was not intended to display virtuosity but to show how the whole body could be used to depict longing for life and fear of death. Fokine said: 'It was like a proof that the dance could and should satisfy not only the eye but through the medium of the eye should penetrate into the soul.' Nobody has ever equalled Pavlova in this solo, which will be discussed in greater detail later.

Pavlova's association with Fokine was one of the various factors which combined to make it inevitable that one day she would leave Russia. His unconventional ballets were not really appreciated or encouraged by the Imperial Ballet. Towards the end of 1907, Fokine made *Le Pavillon d'Armide*, followed the next spring by *Egyptian Nights*, which was later performed abroad as *Cléopâtre*. The libretto for *Le Pavillon d'Armide*, by Alexandre Benois, was originally in three acts but Fokine decided it was too long-drawn-out and condensed it into one act of three scenes. It became Fokine's first one-act story-ballet and led the way to the series of short dramatic ballets which dominated international ballet during the first half of this century. (Fokine came to believe that the old nineteenth-century three-act ballet was dead, except in Russia where it was lovingly preserved even under the Soviet regime. In fact, however, there has now been a great revival of interest in three-act ballets, old and new, throughout the world.) Both Fokine and Benois had various difficulties with the management of the Maryinsky over the staging of *Pavillon*, partly caused by Benois' disapproval of Fokine's shortened version. These difficulties led both men to concentrate on their work outside the Imperial Theatres, and Benois started planning to take Russian ballet to western Europe.

Pavlova danced the title-role in *Le Pavillon d'Armide*, which was set in the period of Louis XIV. Fokine was particularly pleased with the way in which she evoked the vision of far-away times. She also danced the leading role of Ta-hor in *Egyptian Nights*. She was very pathetic in her love for a young hunter, played by Fokine, and poignant in her acting when he was unfaithful to her with Cleopatra. The dances were in Egyptian style, with the dancers in profile and in groups forming angular lines. Fokine found, in a museum, an Egyptian reproduction of a dance with a snake and knowing Pavlova's fondness for animals, he decided to stage it for her. Fokine himself nearly fainted from fright and horror when demonstrating to Pavlova how he required the snake to be held, and he came out in such a sweat that he had to go and wash his hands. Pavlova took the snake without pleasure but without revulsion. Later the live snake was replaced by an artificial one as the living creature's performance did not justify all the trouble.

It was not just Fokine's ballets which were revolutionary. In 1905 he and Pavlova were the ringleaders of the group in the Imperial Ballet which took action in support of revolutionary activities against the Tsar. The ballet company was much more politically conscious than the opera; partly they were motivated by general principles and as we have already seen they gave special performances in aid of the poor people's school at Greblovo. But they also wanted to improve their own conditions of employment. Early in the year Pavlova addressed a meeting of the ballet company in protest against the shooting of demonstrators and she ridiculed the army. In October the dancers held a six-hour meeting in the rehearsal hall and petitioned the management for higher salaries for certain grades, an extra free day a week, and the right to choose their own régisseurs. They also wanted the return of the veteran choreographer Marius Petipa who had fallen out of favour with the management and was no longer admitted backstage. The day after this meeting the dancers were not allowed into the hall to hold another, so they held it in the yard. The speeches attracted the attention of the pupils of the drama school, who came to their windows and shouted greetings.

The dancers decided to strike and Pavlova was one of those who refused to appear in the scheduled performance on October 23rd. Teliakovsky, the director of the Maryinsky, recorded in his diary that he was upset that the traditional Sunday ballet performance had to be replaced by an opera, because of the strike. One dancer who did not support the strike 'blacklegged' and gave information about the strike activities to Teliakovsky. Pavlova called him 'blackguard' and burst into tears; Josef Kshessinsky, the brother of the ballerina Kshessinskaya, came to Pavlova's aid and slapped the other man. Kshessinsky was then dismissed from the company, and Pavlova and Fokine organized a petition demanding his reinstatement. Pavlova led a deputation with the petition to the Court Minister, Baron Fredericks, but their pleas were rejected and Pavlova was told to change her tone. Some of the dancers who signed the petition at first (including the veteran Pavel Gerdt) became frightened and withdrew their signatures. Sergei Legat, who was very popular with the whole company, signed but was later put under such pressure from the management, and from Marie Petipa (Marius Petipa's daughter) with whom he was in love, that he committed suicide by cutting his throat. His funeral became a revolutionary protest: the company's wreath bore red ribbons and the inscription: 'To the first victim at the dawn of the freedom of art from the newly united ballet company'. Pavlova kept rearranging the red ribbons and trying to make this wreath the most prominent.

'The newly united ballet company' wanted a far greater degree of autonomy in its own management. A committee was elected to consider wages and artistic policy, and to try to obtain a relaxation of discipline. But the authorities managed to frighten many of the dancers and mollify others. Nobody was dismissed and Baron Fredericks congratulated himself that the rebellion had fizzled out and the ballet company had been preserved. Both Fokine and Pavlova felt their future prospects at the Maryinsky would be affected, though in fact Pavlova was still promoted to 'prima ballerina' as if nothing had happened. (This is an interesting commentary on the comparative leniency of Tsarist autocracy; it is hard to imagine a strike under the Soviet regime and even harder to imagine that the strikers would be allowed to resume working afterwards. In 1972 the leading dancer Valery Panov was dismissed from the

Kirov Ballet in Leningrad merely for expressing the wish to emigrate to Israel.)

Although Pavlova was revolutionary in her attitude to the management, she was highly traditional in regard to her own status and career, and she had old-fashioned, conventional ideas about many things. While dancing in Fokine's experimental ballets she acquired more and more leading roles in the conventional repertoire and in accordance with the custom at the Maryinsky at that time, she jealously guarded these roles once she had acquired them. In 1909 Pavlova protested when Fokine proposed to stage the *Bacchanale* from Petipa's *The Seasons* as a number for the corps de ballet at a benefit performance. 'Madame Pavlova', Fokine said, 'dances this part in a different production and thinks that my *Bacchanale* would affect her success. Her action surprises me. A ballerina with so huge a repertoire should not prevent others from dancing her parts.' In 1911, on the other hand, Pavlova succeeded in taking over Kshessinskaya's role in *La Fille du Pharaon*, despite Kshessinskaya's protests and enormous influence; Pavlova's popularity was by then so great that bookings grew as soon as her name was announced for the ballet.

It was also in *La Fille du Pharaon* that Pavlova made her first guest appearance in Moscow, at the Bolshoi Theatre. The Bolshoi was not at that time as important as the Maryinsky, and was regarded by St Petersburg as rather provincial, but equally the Moscow public was reluctant to accept anything from St Petersburg. This made Pavlova's success in Moscow all the more of an achievement. She learnt Gorsky's version of *La Fille du Pharaon* specially for the occasion and soon conquered the public with her languorous poses and powerful temperament. She danced a very rapid solo on her points, took large jumps soaring lightly into the air, and led the ensembles with great éclat. She also had the opportunity to show her dramatic ability in the scene in the fisherman's cabin. This started charmingly, with Pavlova miming a recital of her various adventures in flight from the King of Nubia, whom she was supposed to marry. Then it became tragic, with the arrival of the King causing Pavlova's terror and suicide. Svetlov considered that Pavlova's acting touched the fullest limits of tragedy and yet was beautiful, even at the most horrifying moments.

By this time Pavlova had a large flat in St Petersburg, complete with her own dance studio, and she displayed all the charm and glamour—and temperament—of a successful prima ballerina. Marie-Thérèse Duncan, one of Isadora Duncan's adopted daughters, remembered Pavlova visiting them when they were dancing in St Petersburg in 1908. Marie-Thérèse was only twelve and the impression Pavlova made was a lasting one: 'I had never seen such a beauty before. She came into our dressing-room in a shimmering green and blue gown carrying two enormous boxes of Russian fruit sweets (*marmelad*). She put her fingers to her lips and hid the sweets in our costumes saying repeatedly in French and German "Hide them quickly". Then, as we were wondering if she were a grand-duchess, she kissed us, saying "I am Pavlova; you danced like angels".' Marie-Thérèse was impressed by Pavlova's warmth, and by her skilful smuggling in of the sweets while the governess was out of the room.

But Pavlova had a less warm side to her nature, especially when her professional status was involved. Romola Nijinsky, in her life of her husband, said that after a pas de deux with Nijinsky, Pavlova fainted back-stage 'in an uncontrollable fit of jealousy and resentment' because he got more curtain-calls than she did. In her memoirs Karsavina recalled that a senior ballerina (Pavlova) once showed surprising concern for her health, begging the director not to give her too much work for fear of overstraining her. Pavlova was obviously worried about the exceptional promise of Karsavina, and sometimes jealousy got the better of her. When the strap of Karsavina's bodice broke during a rehearsal of a pas de deux with Nijinsky, leaving her more exposed than she realized, another ballerina, identified by Richard Buckle as Pavlova, rushed up infuriated and shouted 'Enough of your brazen impudence; where do you think you are, to dance quite naked?' Karsavina said she stood in the middle of the stage dumbfounded, helpless against volleys of coarse words. The régisseur came and led Pavlova away; Preobrajenska, another leading ballerina, told Karsavina to 'sneeze on the viper, sweetheart. Forget her.' Pavlova was to explode with similar puritanical outrage against young girls in her own company in later years, but on this occasion her anger may have been strengthened by jealousy of Karsavina dancing with Nijinsky.

Not that Pavlova's own private life was particularly puritanical. It is true that humble members of the corps de ballet got higher wages than even the best-educated girls could expect to earn elsewhere but, coming from a poor home and without family connections in the world of ballet, Pavlova could scarcely have afforded private lessons, a trip to Italy and a flat of her own, complete with housemaid and dance-studio, by the time she was twenty, unless she had received help from admirers and lovers. Nor would she necessarily have been promoted quite so quickly without their influence. Karsavina is quoted by Richard Buckle in his life of Nijinsky as saying that Pavlova had affairs at the beginning of her career with a nephew of Teliakovsky (the director of the Maryinsky Theatre), who was employed as a stage manager, and with the critic Svetlov whose writing did so much to encourage and establish her. Later it was common gossip in ballet circles in Paris that Svetlov, then living there with Trefilova, had been Pavlova's first lover and had helped her with most of her early expenses. Her name was also linked with a General Vintulov and she had an affair with Prince Koschubei. Pavlova told Sol Hurok that her own ballet *Autumn Leaves* was dedicated to, and inspired by, a young lover who was drowned while still a student in St Petersburg. Pavlova would not accept invitations or offers of help from all the men who courted her; she sometimes pretended not to understand veiled offers and once rejected an offer of money by saying that her mother would pay for her training in Italy. In fact the money must have come from one of her regular admirers, or conceivably some of it may have come from her father.

The admirer who contributed most to her career, played a decisive part in causing her to leave Russia, and exerted a crucial influence on the whole of her later life was Victor Dandré. He was a member of the St Petersburg municipal duma, or city council. He first met Pavlova when she was 19 and he was 30. She was earning only about £70 a year; he was an established and successful figure. He was instrumental in organizing some of the charity performances at which Fokine created new roles for her, and he presumably contributed towards the large flat in which Pavlova lived. In 1911 Pavlova was summoned to an official enquiry into the accounts of the municipal duma and Dandré was arrested in connection with financial irregularities concerning funds set aside for the building of a bridge. It appears that Dandré had been appropriating public funds for his private purposes, including the support of Pavlova. But the exact facts will never be established as Dandré was released on bail and fled abroad before he could be brought to trial. The fact that he could not return to Russia was a further reason for Pavlova's foreign tours becoming more and more extensive, and her periods at home shorter and shorter. In 1910 she had already paid a large fine (21,000 roubles) to the management of the Maryinsky Theatre for breaking her contract by spending so much time abroad and at about the same time she began to complain that no new ballets were made for her at the Imperial Theatre. She did spend about two months a year in Russia from 1910 to 1914, dancing five times at the Maryinsky in the 1911–12 season and ten times in 1912–13. In 1914 she danced in Moscow, at the imperial residence in Pavlovsk and at the Narodny Dom in St Petersburg. But from 1912 onwards her home was in London where she and Dandré lived as man and wife, and her close association with Russia was virtually at an end.

CHAPTER TWO

From Maryinsky to Diaghilev

PAVLOVA'S first foreign tour, with Adolph Bolm as her partner and with a group billed as the Imperial Ballet from the Maryinsky Theatre, took her to Riga, Stockholm, Copenhagen, Helsinki, Prague and Berlin. The Company was actually only a section of the Imperial Ballet. In her own memoir Pavlova says this tour was in 1907 but it was actually in 1908. The following year, with Nicholas Legat as well as Bolm and a similar group, she returned to Prague and Berlin and went to Leipzig and Vienna before appearing with the Diaghilev company in Paris. Her repertoire for these tours included the three-act *Paquita*, a two-act *Coppélia*, the two-act *Giselle* and a three-act version of *Swan Lake*, all of which would be followed by divertissements. Shorter ballets were also given. Incidentally Pavlova never danced the full length *Swan Lake* in Russia and it did not remain in her repertoire very long.

It was during these early tours that Pavlova first realized the enormous excitement she could arouse in audiences which had never before seen Russian ballet, or in some cases any classical ballet at all. The press was nearly always enthusiastic. A typical review in the Finnish newspaper *Hufvudstadsbladet* said Pavlova 'appeared fully to justify the great fame that preceded her. Her stage appearance is most attractive: a vigorous, supple body and a soulful, noble face with dark expressive eyes. She is strangely airy and light in her dancing, pleasant and graceful in each movement, and she performs her role with an energy and liveliness that entirely fascinate the audience. Her technique is phenomenally developed and leaves nothing to be desired in regard to the infallibility of the toe-dance, the swiftness of the pirouettes, the lightness of the elevation, and the poise and calm of all the slow steps. She represents a perfection which makes no task too difficult for her and gives the whole of her performance a touch of purposeful artistry.'

In Stockholm the King sent a carriage to bring her to his palace. He told her how much he enjoyed her performance, especially her Spanish dance, and invested her with the Swedish order 'Litteris et Artibus'. A crowd followed her car back to her hotel from the theatre and waited outside her room until she appeared on the balcony and threw her flowers down. 'Even after I had thrown roses and lilies and violets and lilacs to the crowd, they seemed loath to retire', she said. It was on this occasion that Pavlova claimed to have received inspiration for her later career from her maid, a simple Russian peasant girl. When Pavlova asked her why the crowd was so enthusiastic, the maid replied: 'Madam, you have made them happy by letting them forget for one hour the sadnesses of life.' This frankly escapist aim was eventually to become one of Pavlova's main tenets, and it helps to explain the basic difference between her approach to ballet and that of Diaghilev. At this time, however, no conflict between 'art' and 'entertainment' had yet developed in her mind, and she probably had no thoughts of abandoning the conventional career of a Maryinsky ballerina. The Tsar showed remarkable prescience, however, after her first foreign tour when he congratulated her on taking Russian art abroad but said he only feared that one day she might be tempted to leave Russia forever.

There were of course dissentient voices in the chorus of praise that greeted Pavlova wherever she went; there are always people keen to attack the greatest artists. The sourest critical reactions were in the German-speaking countries, where some writers evidently had their own ideas of what a ballerina should be like. In Berlin in 1909, *Deutsches Volksblatt* was downright rude: 'The prima ballerina, Anna Pavlova, whose name was printed in fat letters on the programme, is as thin as a skeleton and her ugliness is off-putting. Al-though her tip-toe technique is brilliant and her movements are sure, one cannot get any aesthetic enjoyment out of her dancing because of her appearance.' Similarly *Theater-zeitung*: 'Miss Anna Pavlova, the first lady of the Tsar, showed as *Giselle* her strong mimic talent, her gracefulness and ease, and of course the whole bravura of her tip-toe coloratura. Unfortunately she is neither beautiful nor specially well-built, but thin, like most of her Russian colleagues. That impairs her art and stops the enthusiasm becoming too loud. Ballet-ladies must be very pretty, if one is to believe in them.'

Whether or not the enthusiasm was loud, Pavlova's appearances in Berlin were a big public success, as they were in Vienna, where she had to give an extra performance. However the Viennese critics were cold too, comparing Pavlova and her company unfavourably with the Vienna opera ballet! *Neues Wiener Tageblat* said: 'The success in Berlin could be because people there were tired of the all-female barefoot dance companies which have become an epidemic and also because the ballet of the Royal Opera (in Berlin) is no longer at the peak it was . . . In *our* court Theatre, it is different. Our corps de ballet is almost perfect—that is the reason why the Russian guests disappointed us . . . In our corps de ballet there are soloists who actually dance much better and in addition they are charming and attractive Viennese girls. Critics have a duty to be polite but they also have a duty not to over-praise simply because something comes from abroad . . . The Russians could learn a lot from our court opera-ballet if they attended a performance at the Hofoper.' *Illustriertes Wiener Extrablatt* used the same words as Berlin's *Theaterzeitung* about the appearance of the dancers and added: 'One is thankful for the unforgettable legs which come into sight when our court's opera ballet goes into action. The faces of the Viennese girls generally bloom and their shapely bodies make life seem worthwhile.' Political prejudice may have affected these Viennese assess-

ments judging from the way *Illustriertes Wiener Extrablatt*
permitted itself a general snide comment: 'The male and
female dancers of the Tsar are travelling through towns
where art is appreciated to show the world that in Russia,
besides busy military courts and government secret agents,
there are also harmless people who know how to use their
legs.'

There have even been suggestions that Pavlova was not
such a 'harmless person' but was herself a Russian spy.
Dr A. K. Graves, in his reminiscences of being a German
secret agent, said that Pavlova was paid 50,000 roubles a year
by the Russian government and that the German secret
service stole from her handbag a compromising letter from
a young German ordnance officer with whom she was
having an affair. The German secret service may well have
been suspicious of Pavlova and have kept a watch on her
and her entourage, but it seems unlikely that any information she could have picked up on her German and Austrian
tours would have been of sufficient value to the Tsar to
justify such a great financial reward. It is possible that she
was instructed by the Russian authorities to keep her eyes
and ears open for any news of military movements, and that
she was given some money as an incentive to do so.

The general level of critical appreciation in Vienna can
be gauged from the fact that *Neue Freie Presse* gave only
nineteen lines to Pavlova's *Swan Lake* while printing a very
much longer review of the 500th performance of an
operetta. *Arbeiterzeitung* thought: 'Despite its superior orches-
tration and techniques, *Swan Lake* could just as well have
been composed by any ballet conductor as by Russia's most
famous composer.'

While Pavlova and Tchaikowsky were collecting these
insults in Vienna, Diaghilev was having a sensational success
with his first season of Russian opera and ballet in Paris.
Although Pavlova had already revealed the perfection of
Russian dancing to the west, it was Diaghilev who first
made the west aware of Russian art in general and of ballet

as an art in particular. In 1906 he had mounted an exhibition
of Russian painting in Paris, then the artistic capital of
Europe, and he followed it in 1909 with a combined season
of Russian opera and ballet at the Théâtre du Chatelet. The
ballet section of the repertoire was originally intended
mainly to display Fokine's choreography and Pavlova's
dancing, and the season was advertised with a poster by
Serov of Pavlova in *Les Sylphides*. Diaghilev even lost the
chance of an official Russian subsidy for the season by offering Kshessinskaya, the Tsar's favourite ballerina and former
mistress, merely the part of Armida while Pavlova was
offered the title-role in a projected production of *Giselle*.
Victor Dandré claims that it was Pavlova who originally
persuaded Diaghilev to risk a ballet season in Paris, following her success in Berlin, and that Diaghilev did not at
first think the French would be interested. On the other
hand Alexandre Benois says that Pavlova herself was dubious
about the success of the venture, and deliberately stayed
away from the first fortnight of the Paris season so as not to
be involved if it turned out to be a flop.

By the time Pavlova actually made her first appearance in
Paris, on June 2nd 1909, her part in *Le Pavillon d'Armide* had
already been danced both by Vera Karalli and by Karsavina,
and Karsavina and Nijinsky had established themselves as
big stars. The production of *Giselle* had not materialized, and
the season was no longer centred on Pavlova. She danced
in *Les Sylphides* and *Cléopâtre* (as *Chopiniana* and *Egyptian Nights*
were renamed) and had a big success. *Le Figaro* said of her,
in *Les Sylphides*: 'This one is a glory . . . A sacred flame burns
in her. Mere technique and accuracy in her art do not
constitute her aim; when she dances, the result is that
undefinable thing, a masterpiece.' Fokine said: 'She danced
Cléopâtre with me and *Sylphides* with Nijinsky. She astounded
Paris with her lightness and grace, the poetry of motion in
Sylphides and the pathos of the dramatic scenes in *Cléopâtre*.'

Pavlova appeared in each of the six ballet evenings after
her arrival in Paris. The last was a gala at the Opéra, after

which a French Minister presented Palmes Académiques to Pavlova, Karsavina, Fokine, Nijinsky and Serge Grigoriev. But by the time Diaghilev's company reappeared in Paris the next year, Pavlova was no longer with him.

Fokine thought the main reason for her departure was Nijinsky. As he put it: 'The publicity was all focussed on Nijinsky, Pavlova was almost neglected, Diaghilev lost his best dancer and Pavlova lost an artistic ensemble.' Certainly Diaghilev was so much in love with Nijinsky that he was more interested in promoting and presenting him than in any ballerina. And Karsavina had established herself as a ballerina to compete with Pavlova for public attention and for Diaghilev's enthusiasm. Pavlova certainly did not relish having to share the limelight to this extent. But Diaghilev still wanted her. 'She does not dance, she flies', he said. Fokine's new ballet *The Firebird*, for the 1910 season, was intended for Pavlova and so was the postponed production of *Giselle*. When Pavlova first heard some of Stravinsky's music for *The Firebird*, however, she declared she would never dance to such ugly nonsense. Diaghilev was already beginning his search for the new and the exotic; Pavlova's tastes were fundamentally conservative and conventional. Diaghilev was interested in elaborate productions to which individual dancers were subordinated; Pavlova was increasingly interested in ballet as a vehicle for a ballerina, herself. Perhaps a more immediate and decisive factor than any of these in her decision to leave Diaghilev was a very attractive financial offer to appear with a company of her own in a music-hall bill at the Palace Theatre, London.

In February 1910 Pavlova informed Diaghilev that she would be going to London instead of to Paris. Karsavina danced *The Firebird* and *Giselle* in place of her. (This was the occasion when, as Karsavina later noted acidly, Pavlova did not help her to learn *Giselle*, a role which Pavlova jealously guarded for herself at the Maryinsky.) But it was not quite the end of Pavlova's association with Diaghilev. She danced for him again at Covent Garden in London in October and

November 1911, when Karsavina had to return to Russia to fulfil her engagements in St Petersburg. Earlier in the year, Pavlova and her own company had been making their second appearance at the Palace Theatre, in direct competition with Diaghilev. When she made her Covent Garden début, it was in the title-role of *Giselle*, and in *Cléopâtre* (though not in her usual part). *The Times* was a bit disappointed:

'We did not get quite all we looked for when Pavlova was rescued from the music-halls and restored to the ballet. The two parts in which she danced on Saturday, in *Giselle* and *Cleopatra*, gave her no proper scope. We had hoped to see her as Ta-hor in *Cleopatra*, the part which, it appears, she has played in Russia, but had to content ourselves with seeing her as a Favourite Slave of Cleopatra . . . The main thing about Pavlova is that when she dances, the whole of her dances. With others our attention, and their own, is drawn at any given moment to this part or that; the rest is accessory. With Pavlova there are no accessory parts. She dances with her feet, her fingers, her neck (how much expression there is in the various inclinings of the head), her smile, her eyes, her dress. The drama of her successive emotions is perfectly clear; her changes of sentiment are instantly echoed by little thrills and murmurs, even in the inexpressive audience that fills Covent Garden. That roguery of hers is so deliciously feminine in its combination of full-grown intelligence with the mien of childhood.'

The critics did not care for *Giselle* as a ballet and indeed it was not revived again in London for many years: '*Giselle*, though a big role, does injustice to Pavlova's genius. The part exhibits many moods and conditions—love, coyness, fear, anger, despair, madness, death, resurrection; but it is all about nothing; there is no sequence or motive. In fact, *Giselle* is a good subject spoilt' (*The Times*). 'With M. Nijinsky as partner, she enabled one to overlook the weakness of this charming spectacle of broken hearts, insanity, graveyard revels and sudden death. But . . . the extraordinary intensity of Mme Pavlova's acting in the mad scene lifted the performance to a dramatic significance that seemed almost an intrusion amid the polite conventions of the remainder' (*Daily News*).

Pavlova also appeared during this Covent Garden season in the only two performances she ever gave of Columbine in Fokine's *Carnaval*, in *Le Pavillon d'Armide* and in the *Blue Bird* pas de deux from *The Sleeping Beauty*, then confusingly called *L'Oiseau d'Or* pas de deux. Reviewing this, *The Times* wrote: 'Taken by itself it is little more than a display of the virtuosity of the two dancers Mme Pavlova and M. Nijinsky, but that is enough to make it memorable, for it includes feats of arms (and still more of legs) which take one's breath away because of the extraordinary control of muscle and limb which they entail. Here the pointed toe step, which Mme Pavlova does with an entrancing grace which no one else can quite attain, is used in a new way, with little clawing movements as though only a small thread held her to the ground and she were trying to free herself and sail away into mid-air. As in her famous *Papillon* dance, so in *L'Oiseau d'Or* her art is more suggestive than imitative. She does not copy a bird, but she seems for a moment to partake of its nature.'

Pavlova's very last appearance with the Diaghilev ballet, and also her last appearance with Nijinsky, was on November 11th, 1911, when she danced in *Le Pavillon d'Armide, Les Sylphides* and *L'Oiseau d'Or*. It has been suggested by Serge Lifar that there was a personal reason for Pavlova leaving Diaghilev again: allegedly Pavlova wanted Diaghilev's uncle, a magistrate in St Petersburg, to come to Victor Dandré's aid in his legal difficulties, and Diaghilev refused to use his influence to achieve this. Be this as it may, there were plenty of other reasons why Pavlova was not likely to have stayed with Diaghilev for long, including the lucrative offers she was now getting for appearances with her own group of dancers.

When she left Diaghilev for the second time, Pavlova's place as guest ballerina was taken by Kshessinskaya, who had made up her quarrel with him. This meant that in

swift succession three of the greatest Russian ballerinas—
Karsavina, Pavlova and Kshessinskaya—had danced in
London in *Le Pavillon d' Armide*. *The Times* made this comparison:
'Even with Mme Karsavina it was still a little dull. Mme
Pavlova displayed her talent by making this somewhat life-
less affair a thing of real beauty and interest. Mme Kshessinskaya . . . displays a technical skill which is remarkable
but she has not the personal magnetism of her predecessor.'
It is interesting too, and perhaps somewhat strange from
our modern point of view, that when Kshessinskaya danced
part of *Swan Lake* in this Diaghilev season, the *Daily Mail* said:
'It would be unkind to bring this dancing into comparison
with Mme Pavlova's magic *Swan* dance.'

Diaghilev's company doubtless looked a much more
permanent and established organization than Pavlova's own
group at that time. As it happened, Pavlova's company was
to last two years longer than his. And when Diaghilev died
in 1929, it was Pavlova's company which took over his
English engagements. For roughly twenty years, however,
Russian ballet meant either Diaghilev or Pavlova; as Arnold
Haskell put it, Diaghilev was mostly for the élite and the
intelligentsia, while Pavlova was for the masses—and for the
élite, in spite of themselves. Diaghilev could not bear any
competition, and once gave an interview comparing Pavlova
unfavourably to Spessivtseva. He became critical of Pavlova's
popular approach, accusing her of cheap effects, which he
called *cabotinage*, of certain technical weaknesses, and of lack
of musical sense. Pavlova came to think of Diaghilev as an
enemy and when she was first introduced to Haskell, then
a young ballet critic, she asked: 'Whose side are you on,
mine or Diaghilev's?' He answered 'Both, but I'm on your
side when you dance.' He was right. There was room and
indeed need for both Diaghilev and Pavlova in the world of
ballet—Diaghilev to establish it as a respected art-form in
the big capital cities, Pavlova to show the magic and excitement of fine classical dancing to audiences in every part of
the globe.

CHAPTER THREE

Around the World

WHEN Pavlova rejected Diaghilev's offer to appear in his second Paris season and chose to form a small group of her own to back her in a music-hall programme at the Palace Theatre, London, she was very apprehensive about the project and she certainly had no idea that the group would become the nucleus of the company with which she would tour until her death. Unconsciously, she was embarking on the way of life and the type of repertoire which was to make her the most famous dancer in the world and which probably exerted an even greater influence on the future of ballet than the Diaghilev company did. She had been inspired by the travels of the nineteenth-century romantic ballerina Taglioni with the idea of taking her art to as many places as possible, and she needed to be free from outside control, whether that of the Imperial Russian Ballet or of Diaghilev. She also needed to display her personality and her talent in a repertoire designed for that purpose, rather than in works by master choreographers like Petipa and Fokine which were not specifically intended for her.

Immediately after the Diaghilev season in Paris, Pavlova was invited to England to dance at the house of a Mrs Brown Porter and at a party given by Lady Londesborough for King Edward VII and Queen Alexandra: she was cordially thanked by their majesties for her appearance. It was around this time that Pavlova was interviewed by an English impresario who asked her what she did and, on hearing that she danced, told her to bring her tights next day for an audition. Not surprisingly, Pavlova was sceptical about the prospects for ballet in London. But Daniel Mayer, the agent who arranged her appearance for Lady Londesborough, persuaded her and her partner, Mikhail Mordkin, to agree to appear at the Palace in a music-hall programme the following year.

Mordkin was an exceptionally handsome dancer from the Bolshoi Theatre, Moscow, with whom Pavlova first danced at short notice in Paris when Nijinsky was ill. He was not a virtuoso, but he was a good actor and his strong, manly physique provided a contrast with her frail and slender one, as well as being a great success with the ladies in the audience. He was sometimes described as 'a Greek God'. From the very beginning, their appearances together at the Palace were a triumph. The *Daily Telegraph* thought her secret was the combination of supreme dancing skill with 'a perfect command of all the arts of pantomime, and gesture, and facial expression'. Similarly the *Daily News* said 'These Russian artists are not dancers in the conventional sense of the word. Their art does not consist merely in pirouettes and entrechats. They act.' The *Daily Express* said: 'To say that she achieved a triumph is to convey but a small impression of her extraordinary success.' And the *Daily Mail* had the same idea: 'It is impossible to do justice to Anna Pavlova by mere description. Such grace as hers, such litheness of body, and such perfect balance in motion so quick that eyes can scarcely follow it must be seen to be believed. It is not alone the toplike whirling around on tip-toe, ending in a difficult poise that would defy the efforts of an ordinary dancer, even if it were attempted from an attitude of repose; it is none of the conventional tricks of the ballet-dancer that causes wonderment in the dancing of Anna Pavlova and her no less amazing partner, but their extraordinary effects of movement arrested, as it were, in mid-air—a pause, a hesitation that seems to defy the laws of gravity and makes you look instinctively for the wires on which these graceful marionettes must surely be suspended . . . The Russian dancers at the Palace Theatre . . . will be the event of the season and they will convince London of the supremacy of the Russian ballet, which London began to doubt last year, when Mme Preobrajenska disappointed her Covent Garden audience.' The *Morning Post* also compared Pavlova favourably with some of her predecessors: 'Mlle Pavlova is undoubtedly one of the greatest dancers ever seen in London. For some time there has been a rage for stage dances at the London music-halls, and the Palace has produced some of the best of the dancing. But nothing that has been done there, not the barefoot dancing, not the writhing Apache dancing, nor the violent waltzing, has been so good in quality as this. There is nothing remarkably new in the style of the dances that Mlle Pavlova performs, in her costumes, or in her methods. But everything she does is done perfectly.'

The biggest hit on the first night at the Palace, April 18th 1910, was the autumn 'Bacchanale' from *The Seasons*, with music by Glazunov and choreography by Petipa. Leaping lightly around like a wind-blown flame, wearing flimsy chiffon and with her long dark hair bound in wine-red ribbon, Pavlova roused the audience to fever-heat. It was an abandoned dance, suggesting drunken revelry. The *Daily Telegraph* said: 'It was easy to fancy that the mad revels of Dionysus had come back to our world with the old conquering appeal to strange needs and strange emotions. The dance might go to the measure of a wild Swinburne lyric. It has the same subtle, stirring, eerie power, with the colour and movement of life all but overpowering in splendour. One of the finest moments Mme Pavlova gave us was when the mad exhilaration of the dance seemed to dazzle her and she was languid and slow as though she were afraid. Then at the close, when she fell prone, a beautiful form exhausted and still, it was a new delight to see the wild gaiety of her smile.' Two years later *The Times* said: 'If the rout in Titian's *Bacchus and Ariadne* came to life, they could not outdo this revel of wine and sunshine and love.' Years later still, in Sydney, Australia, the 'Bacchanale' got a cold reception because it was considered 'unpleasant'.

The 'Bacchanale' ended with Mordkin flinging Pavlova
to the ground; the audience used to think, as Pavlova's
mother had done earlier in St Petersburg, that she was
really hurt, until she bounced up happily again. Actually
Mordkin did sometimes drop her rather too roughly and
it was in this dance, during her second Palace season, that
Pavlova caused a sensation by slapping him on the face. It
was generally assumed that she had had an affair with him
and that she was jealous of his wife or of his attentions elsewhere, and this may have been the case; however Mordkin's
widow assured me that it was not, but that Pavlova was
simply annoyed by Mordkin's arrogance and rough partnering. She certainly slapped other partners, later in her career,
when there was no question of jealousy or an affair.

Mordkin regarded himself as a star of equal importance
to Pavlova and resented her getting star billing above him;
he also resented her doing more items than him. When they
first appeared at the Palace they were roughly equal in status
and did the same amount of dancing; gradually Pavlova
emerged as the greater star and did more solos. Mordkin
could be jealous over extremely petty things; once in a
restaurant he complained because the menu offered frog's
legs 'à la Pavlova', enquiring why there was never anything
'à la Mordkin'.

Pavlova naturally had doubts about appearing in music-
hall and many of her friends advised her against it. But it
was quite normal practice for classical ballerinas to appear in
London music-halls in those days, and Pavlova never
regretted it. The Danish ballerina Adeline Genée had already
danced at the Empire for ten consecutive years and in 1911,
when Pavlova returned to the Palace, there was ballet
simultaneously at the Alhambra, the Coliseum, the Empire
and the Hippodrome. Indeed it was as a result of this *embarras
de richesse* that Pavlova found Mordkin's successor, Laurent
Novikoff; they met when he was dancing at the Alhambra,
partnering Ekaterina Geltzer. Pavlova used to rush over
from the Palace to watch them.

The rewards of dancing in music-hall were enormous. Pavlova's starting salary at the Palace, £400 a week, soon rose to £1200. Although she had to pay her company and buy their costumes out of this money, it was still phenomenal pay. Mordkin arranged to be paid separately, and in addition the two of them got between three hundred and four hundred guineas for appearances at private houses. By her second season at the Palace, little ballets were being specially created for Pavlova and her group, and regular Wednesday ballet matinées were instituted, totally divorced from the regular music-hall bill. These matinées were filled out with orchestral selections, solos on the grand piano, and showings of the exciting new 'bioscope', instead of the evening's music-hall attractions. In all, Pavlova gave five successive annual seasons at the Palace, most of them lasting from sixteen to twenty weeks during the summer months.

Just before she started this London venture, she also made her New York debut, first at a private party given by Mrs Harry Payne Whitney and then, on February 28th 1910, dancing the first act of *Coppélia* at the Metropolitan Opera House, where she had been booked by Otto Kahn. Despite the fact that the performance began around midnight, after the opera *Werther*, the audience stayed on into the small hours to cheer her. She appeared on twelve further evenings at the Metropolitan during March and early April, as well as dancing in Boston and Baltimore. She returned to New York in the autumn to dance *Giselle*, various divertissements and a new short work choreographed for her by Mordkin. She also embarked on her first big American tour, getting as far as the west coast. There had been little or no classical ballet in the United States since Fanny Elssler's tours in the 1840s, so that Pavlova's appearances were a revelation.

The nature of ballet had to be explained to audiences which were totally unfamiliar with it. In New York it was described alternately as 'visual opera' and 'ocular opera',

phrases constantly used in her American tours. Pavlova was
well rewarded; she was reported to have been paid a
thousand dollars for her first appearance at the Metropolitan. The critics liked her and her dancers, but they did
not always appreciate her ballets or their music. A review of
the first New York appearance of Pavlova and Mordkin in
Giselle said: 'Every condition was unfavourable to their
success. The atmosphere of the theatre was stifling. The
orchestra was execrable. It recalled the worst of the gutter
bands ever brought here by Strauss or Mascagni. It set the
teeth of the audience on edge, and in the Russian mazurka
almost brought the dancers to a standstill . . . *Giselle*, Adam's
old ballet, which began the programme, is a weariness to the
flesh. Yet over all these obstacles the art of the two dancers
triumphed.'

It is interesting that *Giselle*, so popular today, struck so
many critics then as old-fashioned. This American review
continued by saying that *Giselle* 'dates from the days in which
the ballet was recognized as a possible means of tragic expression. The heroine even lets down her hair and goes mad.
Operatic insanity with its invariable flute is hardly plausible
in these days and even the frequent anguish expressed on
Mme Pavlova's face could not relieve the tedium . . . The
music has a certain old-fashioned charm and there is a
faded prettiness about the action of *Giselle*. Yet it presupposes
that the ballet can be accepted as a vehicle of serious
dramatic expression, and its conventions became ridiculous
years ago when they were put to any such test. Possibly some
of the ones who are constantly prating of the dry eloquence
of pantomime may find delight in *Giselle* but the ballet is
just about as interesting to ordinary playgoers now as
looking over the files of Godey's *Lady Book* for 1858 might
prove.'

The same critic showed a disarming insouciance, which
would scarcely be permissible nowadays, in describing the
supporting company: 'Both the men and the women were
far more expert than such dancers usually are. We cannot

recall their names and could not spell them if we could but it would be difficult to forget how admirable they were in the Russian dances of Tchaikowsky and in the czardas to the Liszt music.'

The American Musicians Union took the description 'ocular opera' seriously and demanded operatic salaries for the orchestra. whereupon the promoters of the season, according to one newspaper, raised 'a cry to heaven saying that it was not opera but oratorio, oblonsky, osteopathy, anything!' This writer, Algernon St John-Brenon, went on to say: 'Ourselves did not think it as much opera as it was legs. Mordkin's are particularly excellent. In certain companies they would be starred. Tacitly, I believe they are starred in this. They received a round of applause all to themselves when they came along with Mordkin safely fixed on to them holding a bow and arrow . . . Mordkin's legs were painted brown out of compliment to the Comptroller of the House, Mr John Brown: for this and other reasons they were frequently encored. The enthusiasm of the elderly ladies in the audience was remarkable. We imply nothing. We insinuate nothing. We are above innuendo . . .' And there is much more in the same vein, which scarcely suggests that the ballet was being taken seriously as an art.

In San Francisco the orchestra which so upset New York was misleadingly coupled with the dancers as 'The Imperial Russian Ballet and Orchestra'. The corps de ballet was 'from Imperial Opera Houses, St Petersburg and Moscow', while the conductor, Theodore Stier, was rather oddly described as 'conductor of the Bechstein Hall Symphony Orchestra of London'. In Los Angeles the orchestra was 'from the Metropolitan Opera House, New York'. While the programme's definition of 'ocular opera', in San Francisco at any rate, was 'an art new to America, the interpretation of the ponderous messages of the great composers through the most primitive and yet most potent of mediums— motion!'

Most reviews were ecstatic. This one is typical: 'To call

what is offered on the stage dancing is to use a heavy, earth-clinging term. The evolutions of M. Mordkin seemed more like flying and the presentations of Mlle Pavlova more like the mid-air gyrations of a Blériot monoplane . . . If this be Russian dancing it is difficult to see how the dancing of any other nation or people can stand in preference to it.'

Having been so successful in both England and the United States, Pavlova was to devote a great deal of her later life to both countries. In 1912 she and Victor Dandré bought Ivy House, at Golders Green in north-west London, furnishing it largely with their possessions from St Petersburg. It became their permanent home for the rest of Pavlova's life and at first she ran a small ballet school there, training some of the early members of her company. She did constant tours of the British provinces and indeed her very last performance was at her local theatre, the Golders Green Hippodrome, in 1930. During her first British tours, her company was still too small to occupy a full evening, so actors performed dramatic sketches between the dances and on one tour the Anglo-Indian dancer Roshanara did oriental-style solos.

In 1914 Pavlova returned to Russia for the last time, with one or two of her own dancers. She was on her way back to London when war was declared and she succeeded in getting to America where she spent all the war years. She appeared in New York in 1915 and 1916, and she undertook enormous coast-to-coast tours of the United States, once playing in a hundred and forty towns in seven months. She also toured Latin America. After the war she resumed British and European tours, as well as continuing American ones. In 1922, with great trepidation, she went on her first oriental tour, visiting Japan, China (Shanghai), India and Egypt. Taking classical ballet to those countries was a gamble, but Pavlova always wanted to see new places and in fact her art proved universal in its appeal. She had as great a success in the East as in the West. In 1925 she left for a long tour of South Africa, Australia and New Zealand,

and in 1928–29 she again visited South Africa and Australia, as well as Egypt, India, Burma, Singapore and Java. The last year of her life was mainly spent touring Britain and she was just embarking on yet another European tour when she died. Considering that all these tours had to be undertaken by train and boat, the sheer effort involved becomes almost incredible. It was estimated by Theodore Stier, one of Pavlova's musical directors, that between 1910 and 1925 her company travelled three hundred thousand miles, giving nearly four thousand performances. Sol Hurok reckoned that it was three hundred and fifty thousand miles by the time she died, which meant Pavlova had travelled the equivalent of going round the world fourteen times at the equator.

Naturally, Pavlova and her dancers got involved in innumerable adventures. The Latin-American tour of 1917 started in Cuba, where the company found itself playing to empty houses for three weeks during a revolution. The American dancer André Olivéroff recalled that they were paid three dollars a day, to include hotels and food. The only way they could leave the country was on a cattle-ship to Ecuador, mostly sleeping out on deck. Pavlova rose to the occasion, wandering round the decks like a ministering angel, cheering her dancers with smiles and a few words. When they arrived in Guayaquil, it was to find disease, squalor and a dingy theatre filled with a ragged filthy audience, except in the boxes, which were mostly occupied by English cocoa merchants. But the peasant audience got very excited and enthusiastic, like small children. One newspaper in Ecuador said that at first sight the company did not make a decent impression. When enquiries were made about this, it was found to be because the girls wore short skirts and had bare arms and necks, and because the men did not wear hats!

At the end of the war, the company found itself stranded in Panama, giving performances in a theatre made out of a warehouse on the Canal. The audiences included high society, naval officers and sailors, the scenery was hung from girders, and the sides of the warehouse were open so that people on the steamers moored on both sides could watch the performances. The crews of the ships were most enthusiastic. Eventually the French Government agreed to divert a steamer bound for North America so that Pavlova and her company could reach their next destination. And the United States army provided beds and bedding for the company to sleep on deck.

In Rio de Janeiro, the curtains of the theatre would only draw back half the width of the stage. Pavlova complained for days, then refused to appear. A local official threatened to arrest her for breach of contract; she was delighted, saying it would let the public know about the negligence of the management and the bad manners of Brazil. The tears of a little English girl who had been promised she would see *The Swan* persuaded Pavlova to dance once more, and next day the curtain was repaired.

Pavlova's season in Buenos Aires started at the famous Colon opera-house, with her company dancing in *Rigoletto* and *Faust* as well as giving divertissements. But they soon transferred to the Coliseo for an independent ballet season, including a special production, as a tribute to the Argentine, of a minuet from the Argentinian historical opera, *La angelical Manuelita*, by Eduardo Garcia Mansilla. The Pavlova company played to full houses every night, but the operas at the Colon did not, as many regular Colon seat-holders transferred their loyalties to the Coliseo. Towards the end of Pavlova's season, Diaghilev's company appeared at the Colon, with Nijinsky, but the Pavlova company was easily the more popular of the two.

In Venezuela, President Gomez particularly wanted to see *Coppélia*. But the orchestra would not rehearse on Sunday morning because its members were playing in churches, so the programme had to be changed. When the President heard of this, he personally ordered the musicians to rehearse, or face six months imprisonment in chains.

In Mexico City the famous cellist Pablo Casals played the cello for Pavlova's *Swan* solo. His appearance was arranged without her knowledge, as a surprise, and he was concealed in the wings on the opposite side of the stage from Pavlova's entry. Dandré recorded that when Pavlova heard the first sounds of the cello, she opened her eyes very wide in astonishment, and danced closer and closer towards Casals. Casals himself said afterwards that when she approached him with those wide-open eyes, he had to close his own eyes to be able to continue playing. At the end of the solo, Pavlova ran to Casals, embraced him, and led him on to the stage for a wild ovation.

Pavlova was so popular in Mexico City that she arranged two extra performances, in the bull ring, to enable poorer people to see her. Unfortunately at the second of these performances, it rained hard and although she danced on for a time, she eventually had to stop. There was almost a riot in the audience, and the dancers had to make a quick escape. When Pavlova went to watch a local revue in Mexico, the manager announced her presence to the audience and everyone cheered. At the end of the show the Mexican beauties on the stage hurled flowers, dolls and ribbons up to her box; some fell into the stalls and were thrown up again by the men in the audience. But wherever she went, Pavlova was accustomed to this sort of thing. She was often cheered in restaurants, and at railway stations. When her company left Belgrade they had to fight their way through the crowd of admirers to reach the train. And in Sydney, Australia, it was estimated that ten thousand people gathered outside the railway station when she arrived. In Brisbane an enthusiast even built a room on to his house specially for her, but there were chickens which woke her too early in the morning, and she could not stay there.

A lot of the company's more bizarre adventures and some of the strangest conditions in which they had to dance were of course in Asia. In Rangoon, Pavlova was billed as 'The Sensation of all the Civilized World'. In Singapore, the company had to dance on a minute, slippery, sloping stage; Pavlova took it with apparent equanimity, but the British dancer Algeranoff recalled that she was in hysterics most of the time. Once there was a last-minute programme change of which she had not been notified, and it took half an hour to calm her down while the audience waited. The excuse given to them was a 'lighting fault'. In India, Pavlova and some of her dancers were invited to attend a display of native dancing which was arranged specially for them; the leading girl was constantly raising her veil to spit into a brass spittoon, and ended the performance by singing 'Tipperary'. Pavlova was so embarrassed that she made a quick getaway. During one of her own performances in India, a plank on the stage broke and only the linen carpet stretched tightly over it prevented a serious accident.

Despite experiences like these, the East fascinated and inspired Pavlova in many ways, and led her to develop a considerable interest in oriental dance. She was obviously impressed by famous sights, like the Taj Mahal which she insisted on her whole company being given time to visit, and the Ajanta caves and frescoes which later became the setting for a ballet. But she also found plenty in the East to appal or shock her, especially the poverty and cruelty, and sometimes just the downright ugliness. When she saw the streets of Bombay, she asked: 'If they must make it English, why not beautiful English, like Chester?' In Shanghai she was so sickened by the sight of a policeman beating a rickshaw coolie until he fell unconscious that she immediately gave away the shawls she had bought, so as not to retain any memory of the place.

In Japan the company had to get used to communal bathrooms for both sexes in some hotels (as well as getting used to audiences which did not applaud). In Hiroshima there was no hotel at all, and they slept on the floors of the dressing rooms in the theatre, along with insects and bats.

Facilities for the actual performances in the Far East were usually rudimentary too. There was the language problem:

technical staffs in the theatres rarely spoke any European tongue. Lighting would be inadequate and the dancers would appear on a semi-dark stage, lit only by the follow-spots with which the company travelled. It was extremely hard to find musicians trained to play western music; some-times the company's trio of solo musicians played on their own.

But even in 'civilized' European countries there could be similar problems. In Germany the music often had to be played by local municipal or military bands; Theodore Stier recalled that the bandsmen stood at attention when he talked to them, and he was asked not to say 'please' or call them 'gentlemen', lest their military discipline should be undermined.

In Vienna, the dancers were not allowed to perform diver-tissements, but only complete ballets. So they invented a ballet called *Carnaval* with clowns introducing the usual solos and other short items, and with dancers sitting on stage to watch, to make it seem like a complete ballet. In England there was a notorious incident at Birmingham when the local watch-committee insisted that one of the girl soloists, doing 'Anitra's Dance', should wear tights and sandals, instead of appearing in bare legs and feet. This inspired the famous comedian George Robey to put stock-ings on the legs of his grand piano when he appeared in Birmingham.

An even more famous comedian, Charlie Chaplin, featured unknowingly in Pavlova's performance in Liver-pool. She was in high spirits and entertained the company by imitating Chaplin on stage, swinging an imaginary stick and raising an imaginary bowler, while dressed in her white 'tutu' for *Snowflakes*. The company had difficulty in stopping their laughter when the curtain went up for the perform-ance.

Once at Covent Garden an inspector from the Royal Society for the Prevention of Cruelty to Animals called to complain about the starved and emaciated horse in the ballet *Don Quixote*. The horse was so realistically made up, with its ribs apparently showing, that it looked starving. For the same reason an American critic suggested that Pavlova's company should be able to afford a better horse.

Incidents like these helped to vary and lighten the burden of the touring schedules, which were extremely hectic. In the United States it was often necessary to travel all through the night by train to reach the next destination; the tours were mainly one-night stands. The company once reached Madison so late that the audience had to wait three hours for the matinée, which was followed immediately by the evening performance. Costumes were often packed while the performance was still in progress, and programmes were arranged to end with Pavlova's solos so that the ensemble costumes could be packed in good time. Shops, cafeterias and restaurants in the United States were at least open late at night, or even all night, and Pavlova loved American-style eating and self-service. She once said: 'America is a good healthy place—the shops are open after the theatre.' In England facilities for shopping or eating after performances were virtually non-existent, but the distances to be covered were not as great as they were on the other side of the Atlantic: when the company travelled from Quebec to Vancouver they spent 108 hours in the train. Even in England most of the day was sometimes spent in travel. So-called 'flying matinées' involved appearing in one town in the afternoon and another in the evening. In 1927, for example, the company visited Margate, Folkestone, Hastings, Brighton, Eastbourne, Shanklin and Bournemouth in one week. Algeranoff recalled having to leave Folkestone early in the morning to dance a matinée at Hastings, followed by an evening performance in Eastbourne, and then leaving again by train at 6 am so as to be in time for the next day's matinée at Shanklin. In another week the company visited Newcastle, Middlesbrough, West Hartlepool, Darlington, York and Hull, and in a third, Cheltenham, Kidderminster, Worcester and Rugby. This sort of pace was kept up for a ten-week tour. During their final German tour the company even gave three performances in a day—a matinée in one place and two evening performances in another. Nowadays ballet companies on tour think themselves hard worked if they give two matinées a week, and the principals do not expect to dance more than three or four times a week, at the most. No star ballerina today would dream of dancing at every performance, as Pavlova did.

Nor would star ballerinas or important ballet companies today consider appearing in the sort of places Pavlova frequently visited. Many of the towns on her tours had only makeshift stages. But Pavlova liked dancing in small places, bringing ballet to people who had probably never seen any form of theatrical art. In Montgomery, Alabama, the roof of the hall had a hole in it, so there was real lightning overhead, and a real puddle on the stage, during *Snowflakes*. 'Never mind,' Pavlova said, 'these are the people who need us and it gives me more joy to dance for them than at the Metropolitan Opera House.' In Milwaukee a three-inch gap suddenly appeared in the stage during a matinée. In the larger American towns like Pittsburgh, Cleveland, Baltimore and Salt Lake City, the company often danced in concert halls and masonic temples; the stages were frequently slippery, there were no proper facilities for scenery, and the dressing rooms were usually several flights of stairs away from the stage.

By contrast, in 1915 Pavlova toured with the Boston Opera, appearing in large theatres, dancing in *Aida* and doing a Spanish dance after *Rigoletto*. But the opera company went bankrupt during the tour and she financed the rest of it herself, at great expense. In 1916, Pavlova and her company recouped their losses by taking part in *The Big Show* at the New York Hippodrome, an even more spectacular and extravagant music-hall programme than those in which she had appeared at London's Palace Theatre. There were considerable elements of circus, with acrobats, jugglers, and elephants on the bill, to say nothing of twenty-four West

Point cadets, four hundred minstrels, a pianist who played while flying backwards and forwards over the stage, and an ice-ballet. Pavlova presented a forty-eight-minute version of *The Sleeping Beauty*, produced by her ballet-master, Ivan Clustine. The production cost over $150,000 and had a cast of more than 500, including the Hippodrome corps de ballet. For three months the ballet got shorter and shorter, ending up lasting a bare eighteen minutes. At the same time Bakst's costumes acquired more and more spangles to compete with the glitter of the costumes of the other 'artistes'. During Pavlova's last two months at the Hippodrome *The Sleeping Beauty* was totally abandoned and a straightforward divertissement was presented instead.

Pavlova entered into the spirit of the *Show* with a will, as well she might, as she was being paid $8,500 a week, for giving two performances a day. Her costume flashed with rhinestones and her interpretation of Aurora also became flashier than usual. She was the undisputed star of the *Show*, and at first she enjoyed the novelty of it all; by the end of the season it had become a hard grind. Neither Nijinsky, who was appearing with the Diaghilev company in New York at the same time, nor Mordkin, would have agreed to work in such an atmosphere. Volinin, her partner at that time, did lose his temper after one performance, and threw his heavily ornamented costume at his dresser. The producer of the *Show* promptly told him to behave or leave, and Pavlova was perhaps pleased to have someone else to keep discipline for her for a change. (The previous year Volinin had actually refused to dance at an open-air restaurant in Chicago, where the dancers had to change their clothes in the lavatories and the audience ate and drank while watching the performance.)

During the Hippodrome season, Pavlova appeared in a big charity gala, dancing to music by Sousa. The composer himself conducted and was so happy that Pavlova was dancing his favourite waltz that he forgot to make an agreed cut in the score. Pavlova and Volinin had to dance through an entire unexpected section, improvising and repeating steps; they ended the number exhausted.

Pavlova made good use of her time at the Hippodrome, taking advantage of the temporary release from travelling to rehearse her company's repertoire. She held three-hour rehearsals nearly every morning and, following a regular routine, the company got itself into much better shape. In some ways *The Big Show* was a blessing in disguise.

Even in London, Pavlova did not always appear in a proper theatre. In 1921 she had a season at the Queen's Hall, which had no front curtain and no decor; the only background for the dancers was provided by some draperies hung at the back and sides of the platform. People in the side balconies were so close above the stage that they could almost touch the dancers. But the Hall was filled to capacity, and the season was as usual a huge success.

CHAPTER FOUR

'The Family'

THE size of the company which accompanied Pavlova on her tours naturally varied according to the places being visited and the state of her finances. There were usually about forty-five people, including about thirty-two dancers. The rest of the company consisted of wardrobe mistresses, a hairdresser, a mechanic, an electrician, one or two conductors, two or three solo musicians to play piano, violin and cello solos in certain works, a secretary, the balletmaster, sometimes Cecchetti, and, of course, Dandré. The dancers included Pavlova's principal partner, a second ballerina, other classical dancers and character dancers for the folk-dances and mime parts. There was a much more rigid distinction between the classical and the character dancers than there is in most ballet companies nowadays, though this sort of specialization is still more common in Russian companies than in western ones.

Many of the principal dancers in Pavlova's company were Russian or Polish, but as the years went on there were more and more English girls, until in the end virtually all the feminine side of the company was English. An English girl, Hilda Butsova (*née* Hilda Boot) danced leading roles in the ballets which Pavlova did not do herself; so did Muriel Stuart later. Two Englishmen, Algeranoff and Aubrey Hitchens, became leading character soloists, Algeranoff specializing rather surprisingly in Slav folk-dances, and Hitchens creating the role of the 'North Wind' in *Autumn Leaves*. They partnered Pavlova in certain numbers, as did several American men, notably Hubert Stowitts and André Olivéroff. Pavlova came to like English and American dancers around her, finding them easier to control than the more excitable Slavs. It was sometimes said that she preferred her girls to be taller or shorter than she was, for the sake of contrast, but in fact Joan van Wart was exactly the same height as Pavlova and she told me that she was not the only one. Nor is it true that Pavlova filled the company with blondes, so that she should be the only brunette.

More seriously, Pavlova is accused of deliberately surrounding herself with second-rate dancers, so that her own star would shine more brightly. Actually she had no need to fear any competition, and she was always encouraging and advising her dancers to make the most of themselves. There were not as many technically gifted dancers available then as there are now. Nor were there as many ballet companies, so the fact that her dancers did not leave to make successful careers elsewhere is no reflection on their talent. On the other hand there would obviously have been no room in Pavlova's company for dancers with very big personalities and grand ideas of their own importance. English girls, being generally well-disciplined and modest, were ideal.

But although Pavlova found English girls conscientious, elegant and technically strong, she sometimes got exasperated by their reserve. 'Why do you always go about with your lips tucked in, expressing nothing?', she would demand. 'Cry when you want to cry and laugh when you want to laugh.' But it was as useless then to expect English dancers to display Slav temperament as it would be now. In general Pavlova was proud of her English girls and wanted to reveal them as such in London in the early 1920s, instead of hiding most of them behind adopted Russian names. But she was advised that the public expected dancers to be Russian, and would not like to be told the truth. By the end of the 1920s, several English girls were openly dancing under their own names.

All Pavlova's principal partners were Russian and all of them except her last partner, Pierre Vladimirov, who came from St Petersburg, were from the Bolshoi Theatre, Moscow. She preferred the virile and heavily-built male dancers associated with the Bolshoi to the more refined and technically brilliant ones produced by the Maryinsky, perhaps because the Moscow men were likely to be safer partners and less likely to steal her dancing honours. Her principal partners, in the order they joined her company, were Mikhail Mordkin, Laurent Novikoff, Alexandre Volinin and Pierre Vladimirov. Novikoff partnered her before the first world war, spent the war years in Russia, and then partnered her again afterwards, off and on, until 1928. The best dancer among these various partners was probably Volinin. He was slim and not too muscular, with excellent elevation and 'batterie'—he gave the impression that he could continue delicate beaten steps indefinitely. He also had a good sense of rhythm and was a strong partner. Dandré thought he was the best male dancer after Nijinsky and could have reached the heights as a star in his own right if he had been more assiduous. Volinin had a pleasant though volatile personality; he told jokes and could usually be relied on to calm Pavlova when she was in a state. Of course he had a temper too, as we have seen, and sometimes clashed with Pavlova. Once in San Francisco, she was displeased with him because of some remark she had overheard him making. She improvised on stage, making it difficult for him to partner her; but he caught her in an unexpected leap and was forgiven!

Novikoff was also a strong technician, but he was heavier than Volinin, suffered from heart trouble and could not always be relied upon to appear. As well as dancing he ran a ballet school in London, which provided Pavlova with many of her girls: later he transferred his school to Chicago. Occasionally, Pavlova was accompanied by both of them; during her last tour of America, Novikoff was on a salary as her regular partner and Volinin was allowed to join the tour as a guest artist, to be paid per performance if and when he was needed. Pavlova was highly delighted with the idea of having two partners; 'If either of you becomes troublesome,' she said, 'I will always have the other to help me.' In fact Volinin had to dance nearly every night and earned considerably more than Novikoff. Naturally there was considerable rivalry between the two men. Once as Pavlova and Volinin were preparing to appear in *Fairy Doll*, she got annoyed and told him that Novikoff was a better partner. He walked off to his dressing-room and refused to dance; Pavlova went on stage alone, apparently undaunted, and beckoned to André Olivéroff who had to partner her unrehearsed. After that, it was Volinin who did not appear for about two weeks, until Novikoff gave a party and everyone was reconciled.

Dandré was very much the manager and administrator of the company. Dancers went to him with their financial problems and their grievances, or just to let off steam when Pavlova had upset them. He was always polite, attentive and correct, but he struck many of the dancers as humourless and lacking in personality. He does not seem to have formed any close friendships though he did sometimes pay rather closer attention to some of the girls in the company than Pavlova thought appropriate. He was generous in lending money to dancers in distress, and frequently agreed to 'forget' the debt. Although the dancers were not well paid, they were better paid than in any other company, including Diaghilev's, and they continued to be paid during illnesses, even quite long ones. All this is the more remarkable when one remembers that the Pavlova company had neither state subsidy, like the Imperial Ballet, the Bolshoi, the Kirov, or the British Royal Ballet, nor rich private backers like Diaghilev. The American tours were generally guaranteed financially by local managements, so there was not much risk, but this was by no means always the case. It was probably the only ballet company in history to have not merely covered its costs, but made a profit; thanks to her talent and his business skill, Pavlova and Dandré became rich.

Dandré recorded that the minimum salary in the Pavlova company was £10 a week, at a time when corps de ballet dancers elsewhere in England got between £3. 10s. and £5. The dancers were normally paid on the 1st and 15th of each month regardless of the number of days in the month, so February was obviously the most popular. There were few written contracts; everything was arranged on a gentlemanly basis of mutual trust. Dancers in those days had no trade union to protect their interests and insist on their rights. There was nothing to stop a dancer suddenly leaving the company, or being dismissed, and this occasionally happened. Dandré's idea was that there would have been no point in trying to retain an unwilling dancer, nor in a dancer insisting on staying once Pavlova was displeased, and so a formal contract would have served no purpose. Nor were the dancers engaged on a permanent all-the-year-round basis but just for a particular season or tour, usually amounting to thirty-two weeks of the year.

In addition to the personnel of the company, a long tour involved about four hundred pieces of luggage. These included forty cases of scenery and a hundred and twenty baskets and trunks containing costumes and skirts. The organization of transport, especially for one-night stands, was always a big problem; sometimes the luggage van arrived at the theatre so late that the company had to search it with torches for the costumes they needed most urgently. Travel was usually by train, though Pavlova did short distances by car. For two seasons she and Dandré had their own car and trailer, but this meant that they frequently had to leave immediately after a performance and travel all through the night.

The usual routine was for the company to arrive in the first town of a tour two or three days in advance. Pavlova was nearly always given some sort of official welcome at the station, wherever she went, so that she had to be smart and poised first thing in the morning. The welcoming committee would include town officials, representatives from various ballet schools and other societies, photographers, and curious sightseers. Then Pavlova would hold a press conference at her hotel for about an hour, while in big cities some important journalists would demand separate private interviews. The questions were often naive and ill-informed. When Pavlova was asked to recount a humorous incident that had occurred to her, she generally replied stiffly that her art did not lend itself to funny stories.

After the press had been dealt with, Dandré and Pavlova would inspect the stage and decide whether it would need some artificial covering (which Pavlova disliked and tried to avoid) and how much room there would be for scenery. Holes in the stage, or particularly rough sections, would get warning chalk marks.

The rest of the day would be occupied in classes and rehearsals. On a morning when the company was not travelling, there would be a class at ten and a rehearsal at noon. Pavlova was often in the theatre practising by herself even before the company arrived for class. Sometimes she joined them for class, but more often not. In the afternoons, she liked to do some sightseeing and also get some rest in her room. She would be in the theatre by six, preparing her make-up, starting to warm up and practise, generally getting into the mood, and keeping a sharp eye on everything going on around her. Immediately before the performance she would be tense and nervous; she once asked the great bass singer Chaliapin if he got equally tense before a performance and he replied: 'I would not be Chaliapin, nor you Pavlova, if we were not excited.' After the performance, Pavlova received visitors as she slowly unwound; then she had supper and conversation in her hotel or at some restaurant or night-club, often well into the small hours of the morning. She rarely got more than five hours' sleep a night, usually from about two in the morning till seven and she was regularly engaged in work of one kind or another for about fifteen hours every day.

One of the chores which Pavlova never shirked was seeing

girls who wanted advice or criticism about their dancing. Ambitious teachers constantly demanded to show off their pupils to her, if only to be able to say their methods had been approved by Pavlova. She felt it her duty to encourage talent, and give advice, even though this took up a great deal of her time when she was tired and would have preferred to relax, and even though she was extremely unlikely to come across any talent that would be sufficiently promising or outstanding to interest her professionally. She normally managed to be polite and poker-faced, even when watching the most ordinary pupils, thinking it better to be tactful and mildly encouraging than outspokenly frank. But after she had seen a lot of bad teaching, particularly in the United States, she began to speak out. On one occasion she told the luckless teacher: 'You will cripple the children who dance here.' Another time, in Denver, Colorado, she said: 'Here there is no talent and a method which is wholly wrong. Where is the teacher? Let me speak to her.' When the unfortunate woman came forward, Pavlova could not contain herself: 'I consider it utterly disgraceful that you ever should have presumed to teach dancing. Not only are you incompetence personified but you are spoiling years of these children's lives. And now, will someone please conduct me to my car.' She could also be outspokenly rude to fond mothers who brought their children to see her late at night, after the performance, when Pavlova considered the children should have been in bed.

But these outbursts were rare. Pavlova even kept a straight face in a Paris studio when a woman, not recognizing Pavlova, assured her that Pavlova had told her daughter she would be a great ballerina. There was no end to the lengths to which people would go in their desire to invoke Pavlova's name; one American teacher offered to pay any price for just a single lesson so that she could advertise herself afterwards as 'a pupil of Pavlova'.

Although Pavlova was always willing to fulfil what she

regarded as her professional obligations, she naturally shied away from unnecessary off-duty contacts with her adoring public. Once when some people burst into her box in a theatre after following her around for hours, she said 'No, I do not know Madame Pavlova, I am Madame Dandré.' On another occasion, when efforts were being made to engage her to dance at a social function, she offered to reduce her fee from £500 to £300 if she would not be obliged to take dinner with the guests. This aloofness was necessary, both to preserve her energy and her emotional strength for her performances, and the work surrounding them, and to maintain the slightly remote image of a prima ballerina.

She was also fairly remote from the members of her company, except for a small inner circle of close friends. Ordinary members of the company were in considerable fear of her, never even knowing if she would respond to their conventional 'good mornings'. Some of them regarded her as a kind of royalty, and were touchingly grateful when she did take note of them as human beings. In some ways she did behave like royalty; for example, she never carried money, always having to 'borrow' it from Dandré or from whoever happened to be nearest when she went shopping. And the inner circle around her was almost like a court, consisting of herself, Dandré, her partner, her ballet-master, her musical director, and Cecchetti when he toured with her. One of her dancers, Leon Kellaway, told me that she had an aura like a queen: 'If she gave you her hand to kiss, you thought it was diamonds.' When the company got off the train at a station it was like a royal progress, with Pavlova and her immediate entourage leading the way, and the other groups following in strict order of protocol.

After the 'royal family', there was a 'little royal family' consisting of senior dancers, people who had been with Pavlova fifteen years or so and were now playing character parts. They had the highest prestige in the company, and got the best dressing-rooms—and the best money. They would kiss Pavlova's hand on arriving at one of her Christmas parties, while junior dancers would be greeted politely, but more distantly. At the same time the whole company was expected to behave like the royal family of ballet, always correct and irreproachable: they were not allowed to be engaged in any public flirations or in any disreputable behaviour. Most of the dancers felt it was a great honour to be in her company, and were suitably grateful.

The company tended to be divided into little groups, according to sex, seniority and nationality. On the whole the men and the women travelled separately, and junior members of the company were not supposed to be too friendly with senior ones. Pavlova was genuinely shocked when a mixed group of girls of different seniorities combined to present her with some flowers one Easter, all signing the same card; Kathleen Crofton told me she remembered Pavlova explaining that this was wrong, and that junior girls should be more respectful of senior ones. No doubt this caste system, so similar to the one which operated till very recently in English public schools, was a relic of Pavlova's strict upbringing at the Maryinsky school. Miss Crofton also remembered being told off by Mme Novikov, who had promised to look after her, for walking up and down a station platform late at night talking to a male member of the company.

The rules of behaviour concerning unchaperoned meetings between the sexes were of course very strict in those days, and Pavlova was ruthless in enforcing them. The most notorious example of this occurred towards the end of her life, when she sacked an English dancer called Elsa Hélène d'Arcy, who then sued Pavlova in the London courts for alleged breach of contract and slander. D'Arcy joined Pavlova's company when she was 18 and the incident which caused her to be dismissed happened about four years later. One evening during a Far East tour, she went to the theatre and found that her solo, *Anitra's Dance*, had been cancelled without warning and that she was replaced by other girls in the rest of the programme. She went to see Dandré, who told her that this had been done on Pavlova's instructions, because D'Arcy had acted in an indecent and immoral manner with a Polish dancer called Tadeusz Slaviski on the deck of the steamer taking the company to Penang. D'Arcy's version of this incident was that she and Slaviski had sat side by side in deck-chairs in the evening and that he had snatched her hand and caught a hurried kiss just as Pavlova and the ballet-master Pianowski passed by. She considered that she had done nothing wrong, and she refused to apologize to Pavlova. Her engagement was terminated and she was sent back to London, though Slaviski continued to dance with the company.

When D'Arcy claimed damages for breach of contract, Pavlova said she was sacked because she had broken the rules of the company by sitting on deck with Slaviski's arm round her and also by sitting with him in the theatre during a rehearsal, laughing and commenting on what was happening on stage. Pavlova denied legal liability but paid £150 into court, which ended the case. However D'Arcy then brought a further action, for slander. She claimed that Dandré had told her he believed her account of the incident on the ship, but that Pavlova was in a fury, partly out of jealousy. According to D'Arcy, Dandré had told her that if it had been another man, not Slaviski, Pavlova would not have minded so much, and he had reminded her that he had already warned her not to see too much of Slaviski. Dandré had advised D'Arcy to write a letter of apology to Pavlova, but she had refused.

In court, Dandré denied ever having used the phrase 'immoral and indecent' and also denied ever having asked D'Arcy to apologize for anything. This gave rise to some amusing scenes in court, when Slaviski was questioned about his conversation, in Russian, with Dandré. When he was asked if he knew what the word 'immoral' meant in English, he answered: 'It means just the same as in Russian'. There was more laughter in court when D'Arcy said that

Slaviski had not put his arm around her because 'we were sitting in deck-chairs which had arms and he could not do so'. But she admitted that he had put his arm round her once on another occasion while watching other members of the company playing cards.

Dandré claimed that D'Arcy was sacked simply for breaches of discipline such as her behaviour during a rehearsal. He also claimed that when D'Arcy's mother had first come to see him, she had not mentioned the word 'immoral' but had accused Pavlova of being jealous of her daughter's youth, beauty and success. Pavlova denied on oath that she had ever made any imputations against D'Arcy's character, or used the word 'immoral'. She was sorry that these 'rumours' had made it necessary for D'Arcy to take court action and she agreed to pay her costs, plus £200. This settled the case.

It seems likely that Pavlova did lose her temper, both because she disliked public flirting and possibly because she was attracted to Slaviski herself; otherwise it is difficult to understand why D'Arcy was sacked and Slaviski kept on. Mme Manya told me that D'Arcy was sacked mainly for her rudeness in refusing to apologize and in telling Pavlova that she was old enough to decide for herself how to behave. No doubt Pavlova and Dandré did use words like 'immoral' in the heat of the moment, though they denied it later. It was surprising that D'Arcy made so much fuss; after all she had been in the Pavlova company long enough to know the standards of public behaviour expected and she could have saved her position in the company by a simple apology. Her mother evidently urged her into the court actions, from which neither side emerged with much credit.

Of course Pavlova, being emotional and an artist and also running a company at the same time, was temperamental and inconsistent. Although she made it almost impossible for her girls to flirt, or even have social contacts with men, she often criticized them for not having affairs; she would tell her girls that they could not become real artists till

they had experienced love. She wanted them to have
emotional experiences, but very discreetly and without the
slightest breath of public scandal. And if they had any talent,
she did not want to lose them from her company. In Buenos
Aires one of her soloists had an affair with the young
Aristotle Onassis, and decided to leave the company to stay
with him. Pavlova went to see Onassis, and got him to agree
that the girl should stay with the company; unfortunately
for both of them, the girl had a mind of her own, and
attached herself to the increasingly reluctant Onassis for
some time, finally losing both him and her ballet career.

Just as she seemed inconsistent about her girls having
affairs, so Pavlova was inconsistent in her attitude to physical
exposure in public. Her girls were strictly forbidden to
change in the corridors on their way from the stage to the
dressing-rooms. Once, in a small hall in the United States
which had no proper dressing-rooms, she discovered some
of the girls changing in a corridor. She demanded to see
them in her sleeper on the train that night, and then told
them that their behaviour was disgusting and they if they
wanted to expose their bodies in public, they should tour
with the Ziegfeld Follies, not with Pavlova. This incident
recalls her outburst against Karsavina back in Russia. Yet
when the young American dancer Ruth Page was taken by
her mother to meet Pavlova, with a view to joining her
company, Pavlova received them in her dressing-room
stark naked. Perhaps it was only when there was a risk of
female nudity being seen by men that Pavlova got really
upset.

Pavlova's sense of what was proper sometimes took strange
forms. She stopped Muriel Stuart and another girl from
swopping their clothes; she may have feared that the exchange had some Lesbian connotation. Nor did she allow
her girls to wear elaborate jewellery. She felt ostentatious
dressing or glitter was inappropriate to the serious art of
ballet, and she did not want the richer girls to show off or
embarrass the poorer ones. She also had definite ideas

about how the girls should spend their money. For example she once refused to let a girl have a pair of her discarded shoes, because the girl had just bought an expensive new dress. 'If you can afford to waste money, you do not need me to give you ballet shoes', she declared. On the other hand, Pavlova did like her girls to be well dressed, in a simple unostentatious way, and they were supposed to look attractive, off-stage as well as on. Their make-up was carefully supervised, especially when they first joined the company, to ensure that it was as suitable and flattering as possible. Pavlova's girls had a reputation for being pretty.

Another aspect of the girls' lives which Pavlova tried to control was their reading. She did not approve of the trashy movie and romance magazines which flourished in the United States, but she found the *Saturday Evening Post* perfectly acceptable. It was common practice for the girls to be reading something like *True Love* concealed inside the much larger *Saturday Evening Post*. Pavlova, strolling up and down the train corridor, would nod in approval. She also liked her girls to be occupied in something useful, like knitting, and they were all expected to use their free time in improving occupations like sightseeing and visits to cultural exhibitions. She frequently provided free time specially for these purposes, and paid the expenses, provided that she got a detailed report of the visit and was persuaded that the dancers had really absorbed what they had seen. Pavlova herself was an indefatigable sightseer and gallery-goer, and she realized the importance to a dancer of studying as much as possible of the world's art, folk-lore and natural scenery.

Leon Kellaway once skipped a visit to the Uffizzi Gallery in Florence, preferring to spend the afternoon sleeping. That evening Pavlova asked him if he enjoyed the gallery and he said 'Yes, it was beautiful.' She then described a particular picture and asked him if he had seen it and he said 'Yes, it was wonderful.' Pavlova had trapped him and said sorrowfully: 'That picture is not there; you are not telling me the truth. Why didn't you go?' When Kellaway explained that he had been too tired her comment was simply: 'You are a very silly boy.'

Her comments to dancers could be much sharper and crueller than that, but these comments were usually reserved for dancers who were lazy about their work or who danced in a way she did not like. One talented girl seemed more interested in rushing off to night-clubs and cabarets than in resting or practising. Pavlova summoned her and, putting her face close to the girl's, asked 'Do you want to be a dancer? Do you want to be another Anna Pavlova?' to which no answer was really possible. After a suitable pause, Pavlova gave her judgement: 'You are a cow . . . but you are a nice, contented cow.' Rita Glasson, who danced under the name Rita Glynde, told me she remembers practising what she thought were rather graceful arm-movements in front of a mirror. Pavlova watched for a little while and then said: 'In England there are first-class hotels, and second-class hotels, and there is something called a boarding-house. And you have boarding-house arms.'

After a long and tiring rehearsal of *Walpurgisnacht*, Leon Kellaway once collapsed. Pavlova told him he danced like a seal. He was heartbroken, because her opinion meant so much to him. He decided to leave the company and go home, but Pavlova calmed him down, telling him he would get bigger parts when he got stronger.

There were strict rules of behaviour for the dancers inside the theatre. For example, they were not allowed to go anywhere near Pavlova in the wings before she went on stage, as this would have disturbed her concentration and prevented her getting into the spirit of her role. On one occasion the American dancer Edward Caton not only lingered near her, but actually moved just as she was going on, to get a better view. She gave him what he described as 'a viper's look' and afterwards he was suspended from all solo roles for a month, forced to dance in the corps de ballet and, to add insult to injury, to appear as the chained bear in *Russian Fairytale*, a role normally mimed by an extra.

When Pavlova was in a fury, it was fatal for the dancer being rebuked to try to answer back or to attempt any self-justification: Pavlova would shout 'Don't talk to me, *answer* me', which in practice meant just saying yes or no. Her pet bull-dog was often near at hand and would growl menacingly at anyone gesturing too fiercely at her, or approaching her too suddenly.

Pavlova was not above inflicting hurtful and petty snubs on a dancer who was for some reason out of favour. On train journeys, when she distributed a box of candied fruits or sweets among the company, she would sometimes also send round the message that certain people were to be by-passed, and were not to have any of the sweets. In some ways her behaviour was that of a spoilt and capricious woman, but really it is probably more accurate to regard it as the behaviour of a strict, old-fashioned mother, school-teacher or governess. Many of the girls in Pavlova's company were only sixteen or seventeen and they came from good homes where they had lived sheltered lives. She felt responsible for their welfare, moral and physical, when she took them out on tour all over the world, and her strictness was not just to safeguard her own reputation, or that of her company. She was genuinely concerned about her girls, and was even known to turn up at a night-club at two in the morning, as a sort of chaperone, to see what they were doing. 'You are all my children', she sometimes said.

Her concern showed itself too in immense sympathy with their personal problems and with any injuries or illnesses. She took considerable trouble to be informed about the nature of these and to ensure that proper medical attention was provided. She always tried to arrange a fairly long stay in one place over Christmas, so that the company could relax. She invariably gave a Christmas party with a tall Christmas tree loaded with expensive presents, such as travelling clocks, cameras and handbags, picked with great care to suit particular members of the company. One Christmas she gave Algeranoff a gold watch and later she also gave him a wrist-watch. She did not like giving gramo-phones as presents, fearing that they would be used to play jazz! Pavlova even went to the length of taking a Christmas tree on to the ship to South Africa, and keeping it hidden until the appropriate time, so that Christmas could be celebrated in what she regarded as the proper traditional manner. When Christmas was spent in Montreal, she arranged a sleigh, with three horses, to bring her guests to her hotel for the party. In Holland a Christmas tree was placed on the stage during the divertissements; it was hung with pieces of Dutch silverwork, individually addressed to all the members of the company—gifts from an enthusiastic Dutch admirer.

Pavlova's delight in Christmas had something childlike about it, and so did the way in which her delight could change to fury if an occasion she had set her heart on was spoilt. Her musical director, Theodore Stier, was once entrusted with the responsibility for organizing her birth-day picnic and he forgot to order champagne. When she discovered there was no champagne, she was desolated, and left for home at once, crying. Stier, accompanying her in her car, tried to console her by saying 'After all, who wants champagne at four in the afternoon?' Pavlova would not be consoled: 'You just say that to absolve yourself for laziness. Please get out of my car immediately.' And she stopped the car leaving Stier to find his own way home. A few nights later she came into his dressing-room, threw her arms around his neck, and said 'Let us kiss and make friends, maestro.'

Similarly when dancers left her company, Pavlova often got very sentimental and generous, forgetting any past quarrels. If a dancer had been with her a long time, and had established a real position in the company, Pavlova's generosity knew no bounds. Hilda Butsova, on her depar-ture, received a Fabergé diamond watch she had always admired, as well as a large cheque and a big farewell party. When Muriel Stuart left the company in Australia, to get married, Pavlova sent flowers and fruit to her cabin on the ship. She also gave her an amber necklace and a large sum of money so that Miss Stuart could always afford the fare to return to Pavlova, wherever she might be, if her marriage should fail. Yet there had been times when Miss Stuart had been out of favour, possibly because she had been flirtatious and Pavlova thought her insufficiently serious and ambitious.

When girls decided to get married they generally left the company as Pavlova believed marriage was incompatible with being an artist. But she quite understood that marriage was a more suitable vocation than dancing for many girls; often she gave them her blessing and considerable encouragement, once they had made up their minds.

Despite the strains of touring and coping with Pavlova's strict discipline, occasional rudeness and cruel remarks, she inspired tremendous loyalty and devotion in her dancers. Many of them stayed with her for years, and even forty years after her death some will not hear a word said against her. After Pavlova and her company made the film *The Dumb Girl of Portici* in Hollywood in 1915, several of the dancers were offered lucrative film contracts but they all preferred to stay with her. Her tempers and outbursts were usually speedily forgotten and forgiven; afterwards her dancers often admitted that she had been right to be angry. They realized that her strict discipline was good, and indeed quite essential, for some of them and that she demanded even more of herself than she did of them. She could also be exceptionally sympathetic, thoughtful and amusing. One British dancer in her company compared her mixture of authoritarianism, aloofness and charm with Dame Ninette de Valois' similar traits.

The American dancer Edward Caton recalled that when the company reached Ohio Pavlova remembered that his mother lived there and insisted on meeting her. Another American dancer, Hubert Stowitts, who made some very disgruntled remarks about Pavlova in public when he was dismissed from the company in 1921, later praised her sense of humour. 'It was impossible for her to be vulgar or coarse', he said, 'because when she tried to be she was simply charming. But when she was amused, her eyes twinkled.' An Italian dancer, Maestro Vincenzo Celli, whom I met in New York, recalled an occasion in Scotland when his landlady found it impossible to imagine a theatrical performance consisting entirely of dancing, without speech. He showed her a picture of Pavlova in her *Swan* solo, to which the landlady said: 'Fancy dancing with only one leg.' Pavlova was delighted with this incident and insisted that Maestro Celli should bring his landlady to the theatre and take her out to supper afterwards, and report to Pavlova everything that happened. Fortunately the woman, who had never been in a theatre before, was entranced.

When Leon Kellaway eventually left the Pavlova company it was because he was not satisfied with the roles he was getting and because he had a lucrative offer to appear in an eastern tour of some operettas. Without Pavlova's permission, he performed a version of one of her most celebrated dances, the *Gavotte Pavlova*. One night in Bombay he was horrified to see Pavlova and Dandré in a box watching him, and he received a message from Pavlova saying that a launch would take him out next day to a meal on the ship on which she was a passenger. He feared a major explosion, but Pavlova took it as a huge joke, and was delighted that he liked the dance so much that he wanted to do it himself. She invited him to visit her at Ivy House next time they were both in London. When he did this, there were a lot of people and he told the maid not to bother Pavlova, but just to give her his love. The maid returned to say that Pavlova wanted to see him; he was ushered into the presence, and Pavlova presented him with all the flowers she had just received from an admirer.

When André Olivéroff received an offer to join the Diaghilev company, Pavlova discussed it with him in a frank and friendly way. She was pleased he had had the offer, and she realized it might be a great opportunity for him, especially as Nijinsky was obviously becoming extremely unwell. But she also warned him of the extent to which he might have to be subservient to Diaghilev; she then left it to Olivéroff to decide whether he wished to sacrifice his independence for the sake of his career. He decided to stay with Pavlova.

Pavlova knew how to give her company moral support as well as maternal supervision and advice. One night in Los Angeles, a friend of Theodore Stier's was suddenly thrown out of his dressing-room by rough bouncers, on the grounds that strangers were not allowed back-stage. Stier refused to conduct until three different managers had apologized and what should have been a ten-minute interval spread into thirty-five minutes. When Pavlova came to Stier's aid, saying 'An insult to my musical director is an insult to me', all the required apologies were duly made.

She also had a good memory when she felt she owed anything to one of her company. Pianowski, one of her ballet-masters, once broke his malacca stick during a fierce argument with her. She asked Stier to find an identical replacement; nine months later, when he told her he had found one, she insisted on interrupting lunch and going straight to the shop, 'before anyone else has time to buy it'.

In general, Pavlova seems to have had friendlier relations with the men in her company than with the women, and she certainly preferred their companionship. It was with men that she played practical jokes. On one occasion she posted the conductor Walford Hyden's glove on to the next hotel on the tour, so that he thought it was lost or stolen. On another she went to lunch in Dublin with Stier and a male friend of his, heavily veiled and shabbily dressed, so that Stier could pass her off as his Irish girl-friend. Then in the middle of lunch she unveiled and revealed herself as Pavlova. Sometimes there were even little mock flirtations; Serge Oukrainsky once took her in his arms in New York and embraced her. 'You Parisien, you truly are unafraid', she said; next day, she scolded him gently for his audacity.

Possibly she was to some extent jealous of younger girls, especially if they were attractive and popular with men. But

Anna Pavlova as *Amarilla (Trustees of the London Museum)*

Aged 9

In school uniform at 15
*(Radio Times Hulton
Picture Library)*

At the time of her debut,
aged 18 (*London Museum*)

Aged 25 (*Dance
Collection, Library and
Museum of Performing
Arts, New York*)

Aged 25 (*Paul Popper Ltd.*)

The *dacha* at Ligovo (*London Museum*)

As Kitty in *Don Quixote* *(right)*
in early days at the Maryinsky
(London Museum); (below) later,
in Buenos Aires *(John O'Brien
and David Leonard Collection)*

With two celebrated early partners:
(right) Nicholas Legat in *Swan Lake* in
Berlin on her second European tour
(London Museum); (below) Nijinsky in
Le Pavillon d'Armide, which they
created at the Maryinsky in 1907 and
danced together during the first
Diaghilev season *(London Museum)*

The Serov poster for the first Diaghilev season, showing Pavlova in
Les Sylphides (Mander-Mitchenson Theater Collection)

As Ta-hor, in *Cléopâtre*
(London Museum)

Bacchanale, with Mordkin
(Dance Collection,
Library and Museum of
Performing Arts, New
York)

A classroom in New York, 1917: Pavlova rehearsing with Volinin, watched by Clustine, with Stier standing on the left and Alexander Smallens at the piano (*Dance Collection, Library and Museum of Performing Arts, New York*)

On the roof of a New York hotel, 1924 *(Radio Times Hilton Picture Library)*

Relaxing with Chaliapin, the famous bass *(Paul Popper Ltd.)*

The Dying Swan: three studies (*London Museum, London Museum, The Times*)

The Dragonfly: *(left)* as Pavlova
saw herself; her own statuette,
reproduced by Doris Lindner,
presented to the Royal Ballet by
the Pavlova Commemoration
Committee, and on display at the
Royal Opera House, Covent
Garden *(John Freeman)*;
as she actually appeared
(London Museum)

Gavotte Pavlova: one of Malvina Hoffman's many statuettes of Pavlova
(*Cecil Beaton*)

Rondino (Dance Collection, Library and Museum of Performing Arts, New York)

La Fille Mal Gardé (Note the elaborate headdress, later replaced by something much simpler) *(Dance Collection, Library and Museum of Performing Arts, New York)*

(Above) *Christmas*, with Novikoff and four Polish cavaliers (*London Museum*); (below) *Syrian Dance*, with Stowitts (*John O'Brien and David Leonard Collection*)

Chopiniana, with Novikoff and corps de ballet, 1913 *(London Museum)*

Two Russian dances: *(right)* the stately Boyar dance, with Mordkin *(Mansell Collection)*; *(below)* a more lively peasant dance, with Algeranoff *(lent by C. W. Beaumont)*

Amarilla during one of her final tours (*Nadia Nerina Collection*)

Giselle, Act II: *(above left)* in her usual chiffon costume *(London Museum)*; *(above right)* in the more conventional romantic tutu. This photograph dates from her period with the Maryinsky and may possibly be of *Chopiniana (C. W. Beaumont Collection)*; the costumes worn were virtually identical. The impeccable arabesque was probably assisted for the slow-speed camera by the raised foot being rested on some form of pedestal. *(Below left) Oriental Impressions*, with Uday Shankar *(London Museum)*; *(below right) The Dumb Girl of Portici*: a still from the film

Ivy House, 1929

Pavlova in typical daytime
costume in the 1920s
(C. W. *Beaumont*
Collection)

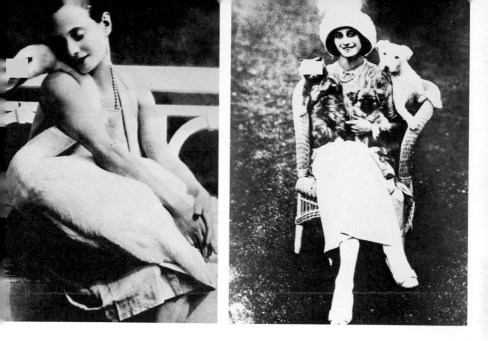

Pets' Corner: *(above left)* Jack the swan; *(above right)* a domestic trio *(London Museum)*; *(below)* dancing with an elephant in the Hamburg Zoo

Portrait by Sorin (*Musée National d'Art Moderne, Paris*)

(*Above*) With Dandré at Ivy House; (*below*) making a carpet for the St. Petersburg ballet school chapel during an early American tour

(*Above*) Backstage in 1929, with Vladimiroff and others (*Radio Times Hulton Picture Library*); the final British tour, 1930 (*London Museum*)

she could also be very sympathetic with quite junior girls in her company. Pauline Barton, an American who was in the company for only a short time, remembered that when she was unhappy, Pavlova asked her who was spoiling her life, and warned her not to let a man do so. Miss Barton did not have the courage to tell Pavlova that she was already pregnant.

Pavlova did not always attend company classes or rehearsals, but when she did the effect could be electrifying, and alarming. She had a very sharp eye and was quick to notice any bad make-up, crumpled costumes, or anyone out of position on the stage. Dancers appearing in a dirty dress, tights or shoes would get such a withering look that they would never risk it again. She was highly intolerant of what she regarded as mistakes from dancers, the ballet-master, or the conductor. Maestro Celli told me that the first two days of rehearsals for *Don Quixote* at Covent Garden in 1926 were supervised by the ballet-master, Pianowski, without Pavlova. There was supposed to be a dress-rehearsal with Pavlova, but she lost her temper over the musical tempi adopted by Walford Hyden. She told him that English musicians had no soul, no talent, and no feeling for music; he put down his baton and walked out, refusing to continue the rehearsal. It was Dandré who later calmed things down, telling the musicians that Pavlova had apologized in Russian, though in fact she had not. As a result of all this, Celli found himself dancing with Pavlova for the first time with only the briefest rehearsal. During the performance she shouted at him in Russian, and he thought he had done something terrible, but what she shouted was 'horosho' meaning 'good'.

Olivéroff recounted the way Pavlova once interrupted a rehearsal of *The Seven Daughters of the Mountain King* when it was being taken by the ballet-master Ivan Clustine. Pavlova suddenly burst in and told Clustine that everything was terrible. 'Ivan Nicolaiovitch', she cried in a shrill voice, 'What are you doing there? This is terrible work. Everything looks rotten!' When Clustine asked what was wrong,

Pavlova stamped her foot and exploded: 'Old fool! The devil alone knows what you think you are doing! It can't go on like that!' All poor Clustine could do was to say despairingly, 'Anna Pavlova, you are impossible. Nobody can please you. I'm finished.' He then walked off. Pavlova took over the rehearsal herself, concentrating on one girl who was particularly weak at point work. She made the girl practice on her points over and over again, till her feet were bleeding, saying 'You want to be in Madame Pavlova's company. Then you must be artist. Otherwise you can take your passport and go home.' Finally Pavlova called Clustine back to resume the rehearsal, and she herself practised in a corner, keeping an eye on things.

Clustine was Pavlova's ballet-master for most of her tours, joining her in 1914. He remained with her till the end, though in later years he did not usually go on the tours, being replaced by Pianowski. Despite quarrels like this, he and Pavlova were very attached to each other. He had been a leading dancer in Russia and Monte Carlo and then ballet-master at the Paris Opéra before he joined Pavlova and he was very good at making conventional ballets look theatrical and at arranging crowd scenes to provide the best possible frame for the ballerina. He was an effeminate man, and not a very popular teacher, but he was personally like-able, and was generally known as 'Uncle Ivan'. Olivéroff suggested that the reason for Pavlova's annoyance at this particular rehearsal was because the girl she criticized was known to be flirting with an elderly rich Peruvian, which Pavlova regarded as squandering an artistic future. She was emphatic that being a courtesan and an artist were incompatible!

But even without being suspected of being courtesans, girls were frequently reduced to tears when Pavlova took rehearsals or classes. She often pounced on girls who preferred to 'cheat' during dances which were supposed to be danced on the points, dancing on the balls of the feet instead, and made them practise till their toes bled. She also attached enormous importance to 'plié', the exercise in which dancers practise bending the knees to take off for jumps or to land softly after them. Pavlova sometimes made her dancers practise 'pliés' for half an hour, telling them it was not enough to *do* the pliés, they must *feel* them. On the other hand she did not encourage the girls to practise difficult feats of virtuosity, and once took a role away from a girl who showed off by doing three pirouettes instead of two. Another time Pavlova said that no real artist would ever turn more than six pirouettes. 'Do you want to be a ballerina or an acrobat?' she would ask. 'You must leave something for the circus. Why waste time practising always to stand on one leg for half an hour? You do many things very good but you do not "feel" what you dance. Until you "feel" you will never be artist, only good machine.'

Pavlova did not require virtuosity from her dancers; she did require them to be hard-working, conscientious and professional. Once in Washington she arrived for the performance to discover there had been no company class that day. She promptly held one on stage, ten minutes before the performance was due to begin, saying: '*I* am Anna Pavlova, *you* are my corps de ballet. *I* practise every day, while *you* do nothing.' The class continued for half an hour while the audience waited, stamping their feet.

The dancers were trained to be simple and unaffected in style, not trying to imitate other dancers' mannerisms or special feats; technique was regarded as a means, not an end, and the dancers were supposed to make everything they did look effortless and spontaneous.

Although Pavlova did not do very much teaching herself, she took immense trouble over dancers who seemed to her to have exceptional promise. She taught Hilda Butsova and Muriel Stuart a great deal, and encouraged dancers like Hubert Stowitts and Algeranoff to develop solos and character dances of their own, to provide a contrast with the classic ballets and solos which formed the bulk of the repertoire.

CHAPTER FIVE

The Repertoire

ON an average tour Pavlova and her company carried two
or three completely different programmes of ballet, so that
they could present alternate programmes if they stayed
several days in one place, or send the scenery and costumes
for one programme ahead to the next place while still performing another. Over the years a very large number of
ballets, divertissements and solos were taken into the repertoire, but in the final tours programmes became fairly stan-
dardized, consisting mainly of established favourites with
scarcely any new additions. A typical programme consisted
of two short ballets and a group of divertissements. In the
earlier tours, Pavlova generally appeared in both ballets and
in two or three of the divertissements; later she usually
appeared in only one of the two ballets. She is best remembered now for the little solos she danced in the divertissements section of the programme, and especially for *The Swan*,
or *The Dying Swan* as it became better known, which was virtually her trademark. Those who saw her as *Giselle* remember
her as one of the most moving and convincing interpreters
they have ever watched. Many people have now forgotten
the names of her other little numbers and of the more
ambitious original ballets in her repertoire. Unlike the
Diaghilev company, which is remembered for striking productions as well as for outstanding dancers, the Pavlova
company is remembered—for Pavlova.

It is easy to be supercilious about Pavlova's repertoire.
Easy, but wrong. Her solos, for example, were often im-
pressions of nature: *The Swan, The Dragonfly, Les Papillons (The
Butterflies), Californian Poppy, Rose Mourante* are titles which tell

their own tales, as do those of the ballets *Snowflakes* and *Autumn Leaves*. Most of her animals and plants died at the end of the dance; only the dragonfly fluttered away. Of course items of this kind are sentimental and slight, and they become almost unbearable if performed by an ordinary dancer. Pavlova transmuted them into something remarkable. Svetlov said the secret of these numbers was that they were danced interpretations of Pavlova's own inner emotions. 'They had neither period nor nationality but were eternal like the laws of life, only more beautiful and more truthful than life, being a synthesis which captured an aromatic quintessence from life.' He also found them more powerful and more truthful than any words could have been, quoting the Russian poet Tiutchev who said: 'All thought expressed is a lie.' The British critic Arnold Haskell said these divertissements were choreographic poems. They were not just dances, but complete character episodes, exploiting an atmosphere and developing to a definite dramatic conclusion.

The most famous of them all is *The Dying Swan*. Towards the end of her life, Pavlova had to include this solo in nearly every programme; it is impossible to estimate how many times she must have danced it. Occasionally the atmosphere she created in it might be shattered, as when a child in the English provinces called out 'Mummy, look, what a dear little white duck', which made it difficult for Pavlova to avoid laughing. But normally the audience was completely held, and there would be a moment of reverential silence at the end, after the swan's final flutter, before the storm of applause broke out.

When this solo was first performed in London, at the Palace Theatre, it had realistic lake-side décor; later it was performed in front of plain dark curtains. The solo itself varied slightly. Pavlova did not always die in the same position on the stage, and sometimes her hands and arms fluttered more than at other times. Marie-Thérèse Duncan claimed that Pavlova's use of her arms was influenced by

Isadora Duncan, becoming softer and less strictly classical over the years, so that the wrists and arms undulated more, in simulation of a real swan. But the basic steps and movements of the dance were always the same; technically it was very simple, and indeed at one time it was taught to almost every girl in every American ballet-school.

However it was not the technique of *The Dying Swan* that was important. Cyril Beaumont told me that the audience was scarcely aware of how Pavlova's feet actually moved; she glided as if controlled by some invisible force. The important thing was the way she suggested the final struggle for life of a dying bird, and made it seem unbearably poignant. A curious shudder went down her spine from the back of her head three or four times during the dance, as a kind of premonition of impending death. Here is Cyril Beaumont's description of the final moments, from his book *Anna Pavlova*:

'There is something at once fascinating and agonizing in watching this pitiful ebbing of life, which ever retreats before the conquering advance of death. The arms extend like wings and flutter feebly; but the effort to rise is too much and she sinks to the ground. Gathering all her strength she rises, her head thrown backwards and her body quivering from the effort. Her body becomes more erect. Again the wing-like arms rise slowly, higher and higher. But her strength fails, her head droops, to peer despairingly from under one outstretched arm. Now she moves slowly in a circle. Suddenly one arm leaps upwards towards the sky in a supreme effort to escape from the invisible force that bears her down, but the figure falls helplessly to the ground. One leg bends beneath her, the other slides forward, taut. The arms quiver pitifully, the body is shaken by a few faint tremors. The arms close stiffly above her head and fall forward on the outstretched leg. Her head drops on her breast. Then all is still. The swan is dead.'

The Dying Swan can be seen on old film made by Pavlova, and despite the poor quality of the print and lighting, one gets some idea of the effect she created: the death is still very moving. One can also see the amazing softness of her arms and the suppleness of her back. Towards the end her whole body seems dejected, her arms stretch supplicatingly up to heaven and then fall again, beating and threshing around more wildly in the final agony. No live interpretation I have seen has ever equalled this.

Quite a number of Pavlova's other divertissements can also be glimpsed on film, mostly made in Hollywood at the instigation of her friends Mary Pickford and Douglas Fairbanks in 1924. Not content with choreographing many of these solos herself, Pavlova often designed her own costumes as well. She created a particularly ingenious one, which played a significant part in the success of the dance, for *Californian Poppy*, a solo set to a well-known violin piece, the Melody in E Flat by Tchaikowsky. (Actually the costumes she wore were not always the same; two films of this solo show quite different dresses, one consisting of four separate petals hanging down over a kind of flimsy, light-coloured night-dress, the other of petals over a shorter dark dress.) First she floated around the stage doing very graceful light jumps and quick little foot and arm movements. Then, at the end, she picked up each petal of her costume in turn, with a long pause before the last one, holding them over her face until she was completely hidden by them. Finally she fell to the ground in much the same manner as in *The Swan*: the poppy was asleep for the night, though to all intents and purposes it looked dead. The dance was based on Pavlova's observation of the real Californian poppy, which does fold its petals at night.

The Dragonfly was a more cheerful, fast-moving number. Pavlova heard the music, Kreisler's 'Schön Rosmarin', played by the composer at a concert and she immediately created this lively, darting solo, with very light, high-speed turns, and with her hands flicking about as she stretched her arms out sideways in the air. Later she designed the costume, with its long wings. Another of her very energetic numbers was *Les Papillons*, which was very brief but which Pavlova sometimes said was the most exhausting piece in her repertoire. It is difficult to establish what music she used: Dandré says it was by Drigo but Muriel Stuart and Winifred Edwards both told me it was a variation from the well-known *Don Quixote* pas de deux by Minkus. Alexandre Tcherepnine said the solo was probably from a Fokine ballet, originally staged in St Petersburg, which had music by Schumann. Richard Bonynge, the conductor, has a score by Asafieff which belonged to the Pavlova company and is marked *Papillons*, and it is this music which he included in his *Homage to Pavlova* record, while Walford Hyden, in his book, said the solo was danced to a clarinet solo with string accompaniment by Rimsky-Korsakov. He said that when Pavlova danced it, she was not just a butterfly but a butterfly dancing with the flowers, and she created the illusion that the whole theatre was filled with butterflies; he added that it was her eyelashes and fingertips that one watched, and that every nerve in her body quivered as she danced. Maybe she danced a 'butterfly' solo to different pieces of music on different occasions.

Other light-hearted numbers were *Les Coquetteries de Colombine*, a harlequinade pas de trois to music from Drigo's *Les Millions d'Arlequin*, and a pas de deux called *Serenade* to music from the same ballet. Her charming solo variation as Columbine was incredibly light, brittle and bouncy; when one watches the film of this dance it seems as if Pavlova was born to be a soubrette, rather than a tragic *Giselle* or *Dying Swan*.

Nearly all Pavlova's dances were performed on point, a technique in which of course she particularly excelled. Her famous *Gavotte Pavlova* was an exception. It was a charming period pas de deux danced to the 'Glow-worm' music by Lincke. Pavlova appeared in a bonnet and a silk dress with a train held up from her wrist. The dance was stately and graceful, but also coquettish. Similarly in *Rondino*, to Beethoven arranged as a violin solo by Kreisler, she wore a crinoline and carried a large ostrich fan. This dance, on point, was all *coquetterie*, and it ended with Pavlova hiding behind the fan, and remaining still in that position. Pavlova actually invented this dance to make use of a large fan she was given as a present by the dance teachers of Capetown.

One of Pavlova's most popular nineteenth-century style numbers was *Christmas*, to Tchaikowsky's 'December' waltz. In the film record, we see her dreaming on a couch, remembering partners at a Christmas party and taking off her cloak to reveal a long crinoline. The ballet showed a Christmas party, where Pavlova danced with all the men before putting on her cloak again and leaving with her true love. Levinson found Pavlova's excitement at the party as touching in its fresh emotion as Natasha's first ball in *War and Peace*. *Au Bal*, to the mazurka from Tchaikowsky's *The Sleeping Beauty*, also took place at a party, where Pavlova danced the mazurka for a group of hussars sitting in a half-circle around her.

Two numbers to music by Rubinstein, *La Nuit* and *Valse Caprice* made a particularly strong impression on audiences and critics. In *La Nuit* she wore veils which made her look almost like a nun, and she carried flowers. Some of the light jumps and falls to the ground are similar to the sort of thing we see in Soviet divertissements today. *La Nuit* was inspired by a poem by Pushkin, and Levinson thought Pavlova succeeded in replacing the words of the poem by her dancing. He praised the warmth and beauty of the ballet. Svetlov said: 'She brings a banal melody back to life. It is a soft, languorous, embalmed night. In the spring twilight Pavlova appears, gliding on her points, with flowers in her hand. At first she is timid towards her lover, who gets more insistent. Eventually she is conquered and gives herself up entirely to ardent love.' He described Pavlova in *Valse Caprice* as 'a little coquette for whom life is all flowers, songs, kisses, joie de vivre'. When Pavlova first danced *Valse Caprice* at the Palace Theatre in London in 1910, the *Daily Telegraph* said: 'Her dancing was the very spirit of spring, all lilting and thrilling and throbbing fresh delight. She was utterly glad in every tripping step and quivering gesture, and yet always with the unsullied fragrance of springtime. Each gesture, each glance of her laughing eyes made a perfect harmony. The whole dance was as delicious as a perfect lyric in its gay spontaneity and its impecable beauty of detail.' The *Daily Express* thought that in *Valse Caprice*, 'these exponents of the old school of ballon dancing met the modern "barefoot" school on their own ground—and promptly wiped out all their "trivial fond records". Never was posing more airily delicate and refined. Every movement had a sylphlike grace ravishing to behold.' And the *Daily Mail* reported that 'Pavlova's indescribably graceful, coy and coquettish movements in Rubinstein's *Valse Caprice* were so irresistible that they caused some of the audience to shout out aloud in their rapture.' Similarly, in 1913, *The Times* said: 'If the audience had had its way, it would have continued indefinitely.' The dance contained high leaps and an exciting lift in which Pavlova's partner held her up in the air by one hand. Mary Skeaping told me the number was similar to the *Moszkowski Waltz* which is now such a well-known item in Soviet ballet divertissements. And Hilda Butsova told me that another of Pavlova's short numbers, *Voices of Spring*, was very similar in its difficult lifts and in its waltz rhythms to the Soviet *Spring Waters*, though Pavlova's lifts were more classical and the music was by Strauss, not Rachmaninov. Sir Frederick Ashton still cherishes a memory of the way Pavlova appeared as a vision in her *Les Ondines*, which she danced with her corps de ballet to music by Catalani.

Apart from the inspiration of nature and love, many of Pavlova's little dances were suggested by folk styles. *Syrian Dance*, to music by Saint-Saens, was about an oriental courtesan making fun of elderly rich merchants who bring her gifts. Svetlov found it full of oriental humour, voluptuous poses, spiral movements and undulating lines. He said that Pavlova was provocative, with her eyes lit up by flames and a disdainful smile clearly showing she regarded herself as superior to the men around her, and he thought the atmosphere of an eastern seraglio was well conveyed. Pavlova also performed a *Mexican Dance* to music by Castilla Padilla, in which she did steps on her points which in Mexico are danced on the heels, and danced around the brim of a Mexican sombrero. In *Russian Dance*, to music by Tchaikowsky and Rubinstein, she was a peasant girl seizing a red kerchief from her boy-friend and dancing exuberantly with it before running away, chased by him. Both these works were miniature ballets, with a thread of plot and a small corps de ballet of character dancers, serving as a framework for Pavlova. *Russian Dance* had interesting décor by Soudeikine with exaggerated, modern versions of peasant houses and costumes.

The only complete ballet choreographed by Pavlova, as distinct from the various little divertissements, was *Autumn Leaves*, created in Buenos Aires in 1918. She had had it in mind for a long time and she chose the music by Chopin with great care. Edward Caton told me that it was simply the most beautiful ballet he had ever seen. All the former members of Pavlova's company speak of it with bated breath. This is partly because of the immense trouble she took over rehearsals; the work was very close to her heart and she always rehearsed it for hours. She also insisted on a final rehearsal on stage immediately before every performance, keeping the audience and orchestra waiting till she was satisfied. She arranged the groupings of the ladies of the corps de ballet to suit each individual stage and she was very particular about them being in exactly the right position, while appearing to move spontaneously and expressively. As the leaves of the title, they were supposed to look as if they were being blown around by the wind, fluttering and swirling all over the stage. Once in Vienna she was so dissatisfied that she refused to dance the ballet, and the conductor started the overture three times before she could be persuaded. After performances of *Autumn Leaves* Pavlova was often moved to tears.

She herself appeared as a chrysanthemum, the last

flower of the summer. A poet was in love with her, and tended her in his garden, but she was seized and killed by another male dancer, representing the north wind. As the leaves whirled in the wind, the poet tried to bring the chrysanthemum back to life, forgetting his fiancée, who had given him another flower. Finally the chrysanthemum was buried beneath the leaves and the poet left the garden arm in arm with his fiancée. Svetlov said the ballet symbolized the conflict between poetry and prose, between true love and fleeting passion. He considered that Pavlova as the chrysanthemum reached the summit of her art, and that the gold and yellow decor and costumes by Korovine were perfect. Even Walford Hyden, who was very critical of Pavlova's musicality, said she showed considerable discernment in her choice of Chopin's pieces, mostly nocturnes. He found *Autumn Leaves* musically satisfying in every way: 'Each phrase, each nuance, each small rubato or accelerando of the music was faithfully interpreted in the movements of the dancers . . . Here there was no chopping up of musical phrases to suit the dance, no liberties taken with tempo . . . Her solo to the D flat major nocturne was, as musical interpretation, the best dance in all her repertoire.' Hyden also said that for poetry of line, the ballet was unexcelled and he considered it amazing that Pavlova did not do more choreography. Actually it is not so amazing; with all her dancing and managerial commitments she scarcely had much time to do creative work. What is perhaps more surprising is that *Autumn Leaves* has not survived in the repertoire of any company in the world. Perhaps it really needed Pavlova's presence to make it worthwhile. But it would be interesting to be able to judge for ourselves. I can trace records of only one revival, by the Borovansky Ballet in Australia during the second world war.

In fact none of the ballets specially mounted for Pavlova's company have survived in other repertoires. They were arranged as frameworks for her or as curtain-raisers to her appearances, and for the most part they would not have any justification without her. Even *Chopiniana*, though similar to *Les Sylphides*, was an arrangement by Ivan Clustine, using some different Chopin pieces, and was not one of the various editions of Fokine's ballet, though it did include his famous pas de deux to the Valse in C sharp minor. Unlike *Les Sylphides*, it had several men in it, and it was sometimes performed with décor representing a formal garden at Versailles. Clustine's *Visions* was an adaptation of the 'vision' scene from Petipa's *The Sleeping Beauty*; another of his reworkings of familiar ballets was *Snowflakes*, which was largely taken from *The Nutcracker*. It included the corps de ballet of snowflakes and the pas de deux for the Snow Queen and her partner, but it also included the cygnets pas de quatre from *Swan Lake*, danced as a pas de trois! It had no story, but a wintry atmosphere which, together with the fact that all the music was by Tchaikowsky, provided the unifying factor for the dances. Indeed Walford Hyden said that 'musically, this was one of Pavlova's best ballets' and that the numbers were so well linked together that the music went from strength to strength. 'The whole was a pure interpretation of music in the dance.'

Clustine's *The Fairy Doll*, to music by Bayer, Drigo and others, was a version of an old German ballet which later also inspired Massine's *La Boutique Fantasque*. Pavlova was a doll in a toy-shop and the owner was reluctant to sell her until offered a very large sum of money by an Englishman. After being sold, she danced a farewell to all the other dolls in the shop, who came to life to say their goodbyes. This little ballet was pretty and charming, and very popular.

A more ambitious story ballet, and one of the most successful dramatic works in Pavlova's repertoire, was Clustine's *Amarilla*. The story was similar to that of the full-length classic *La Esmeralda*; the music was a mixture of Glazunov and Drigo. Pavlova appeared as a gypsy girl who had to dance at a wedding celebration for a Count who had formerly been her lover. She tried to win him back with her dancing, but all she got was a purse of gold. She fell senseless to the ground in despair. Most critics found Pavlova unbearably moving in this role, and they also enjoyed her vivacious gypsy dancing. *The Times* was originally an exception, saying sourly (in 1912): 'We prefer Mme Pavlova dancing to Mme Pavlova in pantomime, and there is rather too much pantomime in proportion.' By 1920, however, tastes had changed, at any rate in *The Times*. While *Snowflakes* was now dismissed as just a display of technical stunts and virtuosity, in *Amarilla*, 'there was more of the Pavlova we all want, the Pavlova whose virtuosity is but a means to expression'. Cyril Beaumont considered it a 'rather wonderful' ballet and Svetlov liked the way Pavlova's role embraced many emotions in a short space of time—love, betrayal, disillusion, jealousy, hope, sadness and despair. Algeranoff found it a wonderful tragic role for Pavlova and he particularly admired her final dance, a 'pas de bourrée' with her back bending to give the impression of fainting. It must have been a bit like Aurora's solo after she has been pricked by the spindle in *The Sleeping Beauty*. Algeranoff doubted if any ballerina today could succeed in bringing *Amarilla* to life, but I suspect it might be just the sort of ballet modern audiences would enjoy.

Like Clustine's variations on the classics, even the classics themselves were adapted to incorporate Pavlova's ideas about staging and to provide the best possible framework for her art. As Levinson said: 'She revived, transfigured and restored life to the nineteenth-century classics.' In *Giselle*, for example, the wilis in the second act wore long ghostly grey chiffon draperies, a bit like nightdresses, with sashes of green leaves, instead of conventional white ballet tutus, and they also were coiffured with long false hair. Only Pavlova herself wore white draperies. Giselle's rising from her grave was particularly effective: Pavlova lay on top of an enormous cross, buried in leaves. As the cross rose up into a vertical position, the leaves fell away and Pavlova was revealed. Mary Skeaping remarked that Pavlova must have been extremely uncomfortable while awaiting this resurrection and it is doubtful if leading ballerinas today would be willing to sacrifice themselves in this way.

The costuming of the second act was controversial. In 1913, *The Times*, while praising Pavlova's mad-scene as 'heart-rending' and her dancing in the second act as that of 'an airy incorporeal spirit', went on: 'We must confess, however, that to our minds, much of the charm of the spirit scene was spoilt by the apparelling of Giselle and the other Wilis in meaningless draperies instead of the orthodox white ballet skirt. Sentiment, we should have thought, would have suggested that in a ballet of Taglioni's days, the dancing dress of her epoch would be most appropriate. A more solid ground for objection is that elaborate technical dancing cannot be fully appreciated when long clinging dresses obscure the movements of the dancers.' However, many people found Pavlova's conception all the more effective for being unconventional.

Two other popular classics in Pavlova's repertoire were *Don Quixote* and *La Fille Mal Gardée*. *Don Quixote* was staged for her in two acts by Novikoff and Minkus's music was re-orchestrated by Tcherepnine; there was elaborate realistic décor such as the spectacular garden for the vision scene which can still be seen in a scrap of film made by a stage-hand in Australia. *La Fille Mal Gardée* was based on the version made by Petipa and Ivanov in St Petersburg in 1885, using a score by Hertel with two interpolated variations by Delibes; sometimes the choreography was oddly credited to the Danish choreographer August Bournonville. At first Pavlova danced *La Fille Mal Gardée* as a two-act ballet but later she condensed it into a one-act version. *Don Quixote* gave her opportunities to display her flashy Spanish style while *La Fille Mal Gardée* demonstrated her ability as a mime and also her lively coquettish charm. Pavlova also showed off her Spanish-style dancing in extracts from *Paquita* and her talent as a soubrette in *Coppélia*, and she frequently revived Petipa's *The Awakening of Flora*, one of her earliest successes in Russia.

In her shortened version of *The Nutcracker* Pavlova was,

according to Edward Caton, the best Snow Queen ever; she brought the part a kind of mysticism, and seemed to worship the snow. It is amusing to note, incidentally, that Tchaikowsky's music for *The Nutcracker*, which we nowadays tend to regard as the best thing about the ballet, was sometimes as little appreciated then as his *Swan Lake* had been in Vienna. In Australia the Brisbane *Daily Mail* said: 'The *Nutcracker Suite* music of Tchaikowsky need not be noticed for it is the ballet that matters.'

Although the greater part of her repertoire consisted of divertissements and ballets designed to display the many facets of her talent, Pavlova was also interested in more serious works, especially those which reflected the culture and folk-art of exotic countries. Occasionally she even ventured to stage works which could be regarded as experimental and original. She encouraged her dancers to learn and demonstrate various national styles, and their solos or miniature folk-ballets provided useful 'fillers' for her programmes, occupying gaps between her own appearances.

Sometimes Pavlova danced in these folk-ballets herself. In *A Polish Wedding*, which was created for her by Pianowski in New York just after the first world war, to mark the Polish declaration of independence, she wore an elaborate white bridal gown with a blue and silver design in special lustre paint, designed for her by a Chinese artist. Algeranoff recalled that she was as excited as a small girl being given a new party frock. Walford Hyden found great ethnological interest in the way Polish folk steps were matched to national melodies arranged by Krupinski. The ballet was danced in authentic folk-style, not on points as a classical ballet, and after a short time Pavlova passed her role on to Hilda Butsova.

The ballet variously billed as *Russian Folk Lore* or *Russian Fairytale*, was choreographed by Novikoff, to music by Nicholas Tcherepnine, with décor based on old Russian paintings by Bilibile. It had its premiere at Covent Garden in 1923 and told a typical Russian fairy story of various efforts to entertain a bored and sleepy Tsar. After all the courtiers had failed to arouse him, Pavlova entered as a magic bird, fluttering about trying to escape from some chains. The Tsar's son released her, whereupon she flew away, leaving a feather behind. The Tsar's son broke the feather, the bird returned, transformed into a beautiful princess, and the Tsar married her. Walford Hyden commented: 'Russian Folk Lore was richly conceived. The use of a singer (off stage) was unusual in a Pavlova ballet. One can only abuse the stupidity of audiences who could not realize that here was something outstanding—brilliantly so. Audiences who preferred hackneyed and trivial stuff like The Fairy Doll were lucky that Anna Pavlova gave them anything original at all.'

Certainly there were strong pressures against Pavlova to prevent her attempting anything too unorthodox or unconventional. Dandré, always the astute businessman, was well aware that experiment and novelty were not what her public wanted. According to Sol Hurok, he had a 'roadshow' mentality and was more interested in making money than in art. Ivan Clustine, who was her ballet-master for so many years, was instinctively conservative in taste, as indeed was Pavlova herself. Nevertheless she made very considerable efforts to vary her repertoire. In 1913 in Berlin she commissioned Fokine to make two new and unconventional ballets for her, and even some of Clustine's were by no means standard traditional works.

His La Péri, for example, first mounted for another company and then revised for Pavlova in Paris in 1921, was set to music by Dukas which was much more complicated than the sort of music Pavlova generally used. Svetlov praised the way she coped with its constantly changing rhythms and he noted that she even seemed to change the very principles of her dancing. He wrote that no 'modern' dancer could equal her understanding of modern conceptions and aesthetics, and that her dancing in this role was original and complex. Walford Hyden said it was so complicated that Pavlova came

to be sorry that she ever decided to dance it! The ballet was
set in a mountain pass covered in exotic flowers bathed in a
mysterious purple light, and Pavlova as the Péri had to defend
the pass against the invading Persian king Iskander.

Clustine's *Dionysus* (1922), with especially written music
by Tcherepnine, was modern in its treatment of sex;
Pavlova appeared as a priestess in an ancient Greek temple,
going into an orgiastic frenzy as she danced with the god
Dionysus and then pleading with his statue to return to
life. It was also modern in its decorative effects by the de
Lipsky brothers which involved the extensive use of coloured
lighting; the dancers had to paint their lips black to show
in the red light.

Svetlov praised an ambitious little number called *Les
Trois Pantins de Bois (Three Wooden Dolls)* which Pavlova arranged
to music by Michel-Maurice Lévy and to a poem by Pierre
Chantel. It was not a great success, because audiences did
not expect to hear a poem spoken during a ballet and
because Pavlova's own role was an acting rather than a
dancing one. The three dolls danced but she mimed a young
girl who succumbs to cold and sickness. Similarly, Algeranoff recalled that a work called *The Fauns* was dismissed in
New York as 'too modern' and had only two performances
there.

The works which Fokine created in Berlin in 1913 fared
better, though even they did not stay in the repertoire
indefinitely and were not nearly as frequently performed
as some of the less ambitious and more conventional ballets
in Pavlova's repertoire. *The Seven Daughters of the Mountain King*
(also sometimes known as *The Three Palms*) had specially
written music by Spendiarov, who told Walford Hyden that
when he was composing it he worked with a turban on his
head in order to feel the atmosphere of the East! The story
was out of the Arabian Nights, with Pavlova as one of the
seven daughters of the King of Djinns. The King did not
allow his daughters out of their château at the top of an
inaccessible mountain. They were sad and bored until the

day when Prince Hassan arrived at the gate. Six of the daughters disobeyed the King and danced with members of the Prince's entourage, only to be put to death by fire. Pavlova, as the seventh daughter, was more obedient and pined away in the garden, dying of a broken heart! Pavlova's facial make-up was so unusual that she was virtually unrecognizable. The ballet followed Fokine's principles of welding music, décor by Boris Anisfeld and choreography into a coherent whole, but the décor was lost during the first world war. Hilda Butsova thought that *The Seven Daughters* and *Les Préludes*, the other ballet which Fokine made at the same time, were among the best works in Pavlova's repertoire.

Les Préludes, to Liszt's Symphonic Poem No. 3, also had décor by Anisfeld who had designed Diaghilev's production of the opera *Sadko*. When *Les Préludes* had its London première, *The Times* called it 'perhaps the most elaborate spectacle which Madame Pavlova has yet presented. A strange mixture of the wholly charming and the quaintly grotesque which occasionally suggested that Herr Boris Anisfeld, the designer of both costumes and scenery, had fallen under the Futurist influence. But of the dancers, of the corps de ballet almost as much as of Mme Pavlova and M. Novikoff—there could be no two opinions.' Liszt's music was inspired by Lamartine's 'Méditations Poétiques' which suggested that life is a series of preludes to an unknown song, of which the first note is sung by death. Walford Hyden recorded that Pavlova was delighted with the opportunity of expressing a theme which appealed to her nature-mysticism. But *Les Préludes* was too abstract and too mournful for the audiences of that period, and there was none of the point dancing which they expected of Pavlova. Winifred Edwards recalled the balletmaster telling her that when *The Seven Daughters* and *Les Préludes* had their premières in Berlin, 'it was very sad, but they were a complete fiasco and I had to wire to London for the scenery and costumes of *La Fille Mal Gardée* as a replacement!'

Pavlova's efforts to introduce western audiences to eastern dance styles were not much more successful. As we have

seen, many critics in those days insisted that ballet should be
a trivial art, and tended to dismiss any attempt at drama or
philosophical or ethnological exploration as beyond its
scope. Interest in Asian culture was not nearly as great then
as it is now. Yet the ballet called *Ajanta Frescoes* choreographed
by Clustine, was a genuine effort to convey Indian mysticism,
using designs closely based on the Ajanta sculptures and
frescoes and music by the young Alexandre Tcherepnine
which westernized Indian themes. Its première took place
at Covent Garden in 1923 and was dismissed by C. K. Scott
Moncrieff in the *Saturday Review*: 'Frankly, a tedious spectacle
copied with a wealth of superfluous accuracy from the
dreary Buddhist art of India.' And a notice in the magazine
Truth said: 'The renunciation of Prince Gautama seems more
like the Prince's walking in his sleep after a heavy banquet
than a spiritual act of great significance. The art of ballet is
not yet equal to tackling such themes.' *The Times* criticized
Clustine's choreography: 'If there is any criticism to be made
it is that in the dances and more especially in Mme Pavlova's
own dancing, too many of the clichés of the conventional
ballet make their appearance. The music of Alexandre
Tcherepnine had plenty of rhythmic character and might
perhaps have been more closely studied in devising the
steps.'

No doubt Clustine's work was reminiscent of Russian
classical ballet. But Pavlova's interest in Indian art and dance
was deep and genuine and *Ajanta Frescoes* was only one of
three Indian ballets which had premières during her brief
Covent Garden season in 1923. *Ajanta Frescoes* derived from
her emotion when she saw the Ajanta temple and caves,
and the second Indian ballet, *Hindu Wedding*, was suggested
to her when she saw a wedding ceremony in Bombay.
Algeranoff was sent to the Victoria and Albert Museum in
London to research on Indian wedding customs and his
cousin made enlarged copies of prints of Indian costumes
from the British Museum. O. Allegri based his designs on
these. Pavlova also asked Algeranoff to go to a recital of

Indian music given in London by Commalata Bannarjee, a recital which had important repercussions both for Pavlova and for Indian dance.

Algeranoff's favourable report on the music led Pavlova to invite Miss Bannarjee to give a recital at Ivy House, and Pavlova was then so delighted that she asked her to write the score for *Hindu Wedding*. Miss Bannarjee introduced · Pavlova to the young Uday Shankar who was studying painting at the Royal College of Arts in London under Sir William Rothenstein. Shankar had already studied Indian dancing and was just beginning to perform in public. Pavlova eventually asked him to make two ballets for her, *Hindu Wedding* and a Radha-Krishna duet, both of which were incorporated in a work called *Oriental Impressions*. Shankar worked with Pavlova and her company for three months, teaching them Indian-style movements. He himself danced Krishna to Pavlova's Radha. In this pas de deux, for which Miss Bannarjee also wrote the music, Pavlova was all gentle submissiveness to Shankar's handsome lover-god. The costumes were made of genuine Indian fabrics, and the dancing was obviously more authentic than in *Ajanta Frescoes*. The ballet was not a great success in London though it was popular with the Indian community; it was more successful in the United States and was actually greatly admired when Pavlova plucked up her courage to present it in India during her 1928-29 tour.

Pavlova toured with Shankar as her partner for nine months, in Canada, Mexico and all over the United States. Edward Caton said that she was amazingly transformed when dancing with him—'she became an oriental dancer'. Later Shankar wrote: 'During my travels, I watched her troupe and found how hard they worked. To them, work was like their God. This was indeed a lesson for me. I saw how they concentrated on organization, discipline, and above all, showmanship.' Pavlova encouraged Shankar to persevere with his dancing, dissuading him from trying to learn western classical ballet and urging him to develop the music and dances of his own country and to bring them to the west. 'I kept to her advice from that day for ever', he said. After leaving Pavlova, Shankar studied in Paris before returning to India to form his own company, which then toured the world off and on for about thirty years.

Another great Indian dancer, Ram Gopal, has pointed out that Indian dancing was dead or dying when Pavlova first took an interest in it. Very little was being performed, and such dancers as there were often seemed slovenly and unauthentic. Gopal considered that *Ajanta Frescoes*, *Radha and Krishna* and *Hindu Wedding* marvellously captured the inner spirit of India and that without Pavlova there might not have been the great revival of Hindu dance, which now flourishes in India and all over the world. She not only inspired Shankar to do his creative work but later she also gave newspaper interviews in India stressing the potential importance of Indian dance. She suggested to Algeranoff, who had taken over Shankar's role of Krishna, that he should do a joint recital with an Indian dancer called Menaka. Pavlova attended the recital and praised Menaka, telling her to make Indian ballets of her own. Menaka did this and had a big success both in Europe and in India in the 1930s. A stranger tribute to Pavlova's influence in India was a lady called Rukmini Devi who not only revived erotic Indian temple dances but even learnt *The Dying Swan* and performed it regularly at theosophic conventions!

Pavlova's interest in the east was not limited to India. When she toured Japan she instinctively understood and appreciated *Noh* drama and she hired a Japanese lady to travel with the company and teach them local movement styles and dances. In particular she encouraged Algeranoff to learn several Japanese solos, including one which was really intended for females. Algeranoff's knowledge was put to good use in *Oriental Impressions*, which included a Japanese scene as well as the two Indian ones. He danced to special music with Japanese effects, arranged for a western orchestra by Henry Gheel. Pavlova herself had learnt some Japanese dances but she felt they were bad for her legs and she did not perform them in public. Instead she sometimes appeared in the Japanese section of *Oriental Impressions* as a Japanese butterfly, doing one of her typical light, fluttery numbers to Grieg's 'Butterfly Dance'. The appalling Japanese earthquake of 1923 which killed around 90,000 people took place during the London rehearsals of this ballet, and the £600 profit on the Covent Garden première was given to the Lord Mayor's earthquake relief fund. The Japanese Ambassador attended the performance and thanked Pavlova on stage, presenting her with a bouquet; Japanese ladies in kimonos sold programmes. Later in the same year, the Japanese section of *Oriental Impressions* got less sympathy in the United States, because the Americans were becoming conscious of the 'yellow peril'.

Pavlova also did an *Egyptian Ballet* to agreeable but not very Egyptian music by Luigini, sometimes augmented with the march from Verdi's *Aida* and an Egyptian waltz by Arensky and for a short time she performed a story-ballet variously titled *The Egyptian Mummy* and *The Romance of a Mummy* with a specially commissioned score by Nicholas Tcherepnine. This was a dramatic ballet in three scenes about a Pharaoh's daughter being resurrected from a sarcophagus by an archaeologist. The choreography of both Egyptian ballets was credited to Clustine, but some members of the company remember the *Mummy* ballet being rehearsed by Novikoff. Although Pavlova danced classically, on her points, she included Egyptian-style arm movements which she copied from ancient Egyptian friezes and papyri.

Pavlova never staged a ballet with a British or North American setting, though she did express interest in both ideas. In an article in the *Strand Magazine* in October 1913, she wrote: 'I can see infinite possibilities in the Highland fling and reels. Moreover one has always the charm and picturesqueness of the costume . . . I can see the Scottish ballet wonderfully clearly. I can see it all—the village in the purple glen, the grey church in the distance. And the story? That would be the old story of the village maiden about to marry one of her own class. Of course she loves the Laird of the Manor dressed as a shepherd. The complications are apparent and one could weave the ballet dances of a fantastic as well as a realistic nature. I have heard some of the Scottish folk-songs and these I find both charming and mystical, and for this reason they would I think make an excellent foundation for a great artistic ballet. As far as Scottish dancing is concerned, I have always thought that it bears a greater resemblance to the tarantella of Italy than anything else. On occasions I have heard Scottish dancing compared to Russian dancing but frankly I can find no point of resemblance between the styles of the two countries.' It is quite possible that Pavlova had never seen Bournonville's *La Sylphide*, which is similar to the kind of ballet she had in mind.

Three years later, in September 1916, Pavlova published an article in the New York *Sun* in almost identical terms, this time envisaging a ballet with a native American setting. 'The longer I remain in America the more convinced I am that there lie distinct possibilities in an entirely American ballet', she wrote. 'I have often dreamed of an American ballet, because I can see infinite possibilities in the action and vitality of the native dances . . . Last season in the arrangement made by Sousa for the Hippodrome's ballet of the States there was an absolute thrill in "Dixie", "Maryland", "Colorado", "California" and other melodies . . . I can see it all—the grandeur of the West, the romance of the South, the pastoral beauty of the East.' Clearly Pavlova saw no inherent reason why she should not stage British and American folk-ballets, just as she staged eastern ones.

One might have expected, and Pavlova clearly hoped, that her exotic oriental ballets would appeal to western audiences in exactly the same way as Russian folk-lore ballets like *Petrouchka* and *The Firebird*, brought to Paris and London by Diaghilev. But apart from the fact that Pavlova's collaborators were not as distinguished as Fokine and

Stravinsky, her audience was entirely different from Diaghilev's. The difference was astutely noted and reported in an article in the London *Evening Standard* by Philip Page in 1927. He wrote:

'Mme Pavlova's season of ballet at Covent Garden (which is being very well supported even at matinées, when ballet of any kind is an acquired taste), coming only a few weeks after the close of the Diaghilev troupe's visit to the Princes Theatre, gives an opportunity for studying two opposite types of the ballet entertainment, both of which have a large following. The audiences for each overlap not at all. One does not see at Covent Garden the ecstatic youth with flowing hair who expresses his appreciation of Serge Lifar with a mass of sibilants ... The superficial view is to declare that Diaghilev is progressive and Pavlova, whose ballets are admittedly old-fashioned, reactionary. But this is not true, and hardly fair to the latter ... Ballet owes an immense debt to Pavlova simply because she concentrates on the best dancing in the traditional style which might otherwise be in danger of becoming choked by continuous striving after the bizarre because it is modern or after the ugly because it is ugly.'

How apt those remarks are today, both about ballet audiences and about some of the works which we are now expected to admire. But a great deal of the kind of experimentation which we see today in so-called 'modern dance' and 'avant-garde ballet' was already happening in Pavlova's day, and she held very decided views about it. Although she had cooperated with Fokine in some of his experiments, and had commissioned *Les Préludes* and *The Seven Daughters of the Mountain King* from him, she had reservations about his work. She once said: 'He is a man of genius ... Yet the beauty of the scenes he combines, the splendours of the settings and costumes, the charm of the music, exercise so captivating an effect upon the public that the dancer's individuality is lost sight of.' Nothing could put more clearly her opposition to the Diaghilev-Fokine belief that dancing, décor, music and story should all be ingredients of equal importance in a ballet; for Pavlova, everything else was subordinate to the dancing, and to her dancing in particular.

Although Pavlova's and Fokine's ways parted, she always retained a respect for him. Both of them believed in progress through evolution rather than revolution and neither of them was interested in deliberately trying to shock an audience or in being grotesque so as to seem 'modern'. As Diaghilev's productions went further and further in that direction, Pavlova became more and more hostile to them. On one occasion when Diaghilev tried to persuade her to rejoin his company, she was tempted to do so but insisted that Fokine must also be engaged as artistic director. By that time, however, Diaghilev had other, more 'progressive' choreographers. Pavlova was even shocked by the ending of Massine's *La Boutique Fantasque*, which now seems extraordinarily conventional, because the girls were held upside-down, showing their legs right up to their waists. As for Massine's factory ballet, *Pas d'Acier*, it forced Pavlova to leave the theatre and upset her for days. 'Where is the art in all this?' she asked.

Pavlova was not against new ideas or new techniques being brought into ballet, but she was against ugliness, sensationalism and performances which used dancers as acrobats. She was aware of her own pure classical style having been modified by the freer movement developed by Isadora Duncan; in an article called 'An Answer to Critics of the Ballet' published in the American magazine *The Dance* in 1926, she wrote: 'It was the dancing of the natural school which brought freedom to the old-time ballet, for we added to our ancient technique the abandon and classic beauty of Isadora Duncan's sublime art, augmenting the power and sensitiveness of our instrument.' But she was impatient of the idea that natural movement, without precise technique, was enough. And, in the same article, she put up a reasoned defence of the artificiality of point-dancing, a defence which is just as valid today when ballet is sometimes attacked as outmoded and unrealistic. Pavlova's article is worth quoting fairly extensively:

'The purpose of dancing is not to show men as they look when they go about their work, a little grubby, a little sordid, a little pathetic. Contrarily, the function of dancing is to give man a sight of an unreal world, beautiful, dazzling as his dreams. For dancing is pure romance and it is by the grace of romance that man sees himself, not as he is, but as he should like to be . . . beautiful, free, healthy, happy, carefree . . . Man has always envied birds and angels their power of flight. Man has always aspired to rise physically to as great heights as his emotions have lifted him. It is only with the help of cumbersome machinery that man can leave the surface of the earth and rise high into the air; and there is very little spiritual satisfaction in being hurled through space in an aeroplane. It was through this desire to experience and express the beauty and freedom of flight that the toe technique was born. The dancer desired to be more than merely human. The dancer wished to express above all other things that surging, rising, uplifted feeling of a great emotion. And so the old masters contrived the technique of the pointed toe by means of which the body was able to serve as a symbol for the spirit . . . Today the ballet is a fantastic and complex art. Through years of arduous practice its disciple learns to make his or her body an instrument at once strong and sensitive, powerful and delicate, voluptuous and ethereal. An instrument of un-limited versatility, capable of the swiftest movement, able to express the darkest tragedy at one moment and the brightest comedy the next. Passion and chastity, awe and audacity, abandon and restraint, fear and courage, all must be within the powers of this mobile instrument. Each age, each land, each era of human thought must be within the comprehension and expression of the dancer of the ballet . . . And the 'natural' movements of the body are not enough to express the range of emotions and the changes of time and scene which its drama presents. The 'natural' schools cannot be so versatile. Their art is easier to acquire, but it is only the rare genius who can convey genuine feeling through its simple movements. Unless the fire is present, the poses sink to mere banality . . .

'Nor do I mean to say that technique alone is sufficient in the ballet of the pointed toe . . . Merely to use the toe technique as an exhibit of strength and skill is to defeat the purpose of the dance. Such demonstrations are all very well in the circus, but they are in execrable taste on the stage. Two pirouettes graciously executed are better than twelve performed as if the dancer were desperately anxious to exhibit her skill. A soft movement, a passionate movement, is better than a difficult movement, for the purpose of a dance is not to elicit a gasp of wonder from the audience, but to give the spectators a flashing glimpse of potent and dazzling beauty.

'Art is not merely a medium for catering to the whims of one generation or of portraying life as it is. Art is prayer, love, religion. Art expresses the need for greater freedom than mortals possess and greater goodness than is known to man. If these things can be conveyed by "naturalness", then "naturalness" is art. But if something more than natural is necessary to tell of the flight of fancy, of the fabric of dreams, of the bright surging of joyous thoughts, of our wonder and delight in the magnificence of the universe, of our grasping towards the stars, and if that something successfully expresses these strange and remote desires, certainly it is Art.'

In December of the same year, 1926, she expressed similar thoughts, laced with optimism about the future, in an article in the *Strand Magazine*: 'The impulse for unpopular and ungraceful forms of dancing is already on the wane, just as is the demand for Cubist paintings. And in a few years I think that only those which are really beautiful and graceful will remain . . . It is by the steady elimination of everything which is ugly—thoughts and deeds no less than tangible things—and by the substitution of others of true and lasting beauty that the whole progress of humanity proceeds.'

Pavlova was right in her short-term prediction about avant-garde art, though her ideal that all dancing should be beautiful and graceful is out of fashion again now. But despite her perhaps rather sentimental view of art, and her hostility to much of the experiment that was going on around her, she could appreciate some 'modern' dancers, just as her sensitivity and emotional warmth were appreciated by devotees of 'modern' dance who generally criticized classical ballerinas for being stiff and artificial. In Berlin in 1925, where the 'modern' school of Mary Wigman was all the rage, Wigman's followers admired Pavlova's 'soft' lyrical arms. In her turn Pavlova was interested in what Wigman and Isadora Duncan were doing, and Sol Hurok has recalled that she was the first person to urge him to see their work. At the same time Pavlova realized that many of the 'experiments' around her echoed Fokine's experiments of 1910, and she knew that while a well-trained classical dancer could do all the Wigman and Duncan movments, a 'modern' dancer could not possibly master classical steps. When Pavlova and Wigman met in Dresden, Wigman offered to allow Pavlova to perform one of her dances. Pavlova coolly and politely replied that she would do one of Wigman's if Wigman would do one of hers!

Just as Pavlova tried to keep her eyes open to new techniques, she also tried to keep an ear open for new music, though most of it did not appeal to her personally. She was conservative in her taste, and very conscious of the importance of preserving work which had been proved over the years. As we have seen, most of the music in her repertoire was traditional and rather old-fashioned. She liked tuneful, lyrical music that accompanied the dance and helped her to express emotions and moods; in other words she preferred a clear melody, with a strong feeling, to music which relied mainly on rhythm. And she did not like to use serious symphonic music to which she would have had to adapt herself; she required music which could be adapted to her. In an interview printed in the *Sydney Morning Herald* in 1929 she said: 'So far as new music is concerned, I do not oppose it, by any means. But I say this, we must be cautious about it. We are living in a transient age, an age of experiment. Art must mean more to the people than a mere search for amusement, or mere experiments in new forms; and our duty is to preserve the pure standards of art, and the sincerity of art. Therefore the new forms must be proved.'

At one time Pavlova even considered the idea of making a ballet without any music at all, an idea which only gained acceptance in comparatively avant-garde circles in our own time, half a century later. In an interview in the *New York Times* in 1915 she was quoted as saying: 'It has been my dream to perfect the dancing of myself and my company to the extent that music should become only an accentuation instead of a dominating factor . . . I am planning to try the experiment of a ballet without music one day. Of course it would have to be before an invited audience, for the innovation would be too radical to attract the masses.'

Among the new forms which Pavlova particularly disliked, regarding them as signs of decadence, were jazz and the sort of dances that went with it. Theodore Stier quoted her views on jazz as follows: 'It is the very lowest form of amusement, and one for which I have nothing but the most supreme contempt. It is entirely without beauty; the music is a very horrible noise made by instruments that are raucous in the extreme and which emit only an intensified form of savage rhythm. Furthermore, as far as concerns the dancing, there is in it a pretence of harmlessness which in reality contains an underlying viciousness that is calculated to cause an infinity of harm.' And in an interview published in the *Toledo News* in 1921, she said: 'The way a nation dances indicates its character and moral fibre. That is why dances like the shimmy, the Chicago and the toddle—which have their counterparts in England, France, Germany and other European countries—are so deplorable. They are the manifestations of the spirit of recklessness and the letting down of moral forces which characterize our time.'

Later, however, she became a bit more tolerant. In her 1926 article in the *Strand Magazine* she made allowances and excuses for the 'absolute abandon' of jazz dancing: 'We all know this to be a form of modern dancing which is a typical reflection of the desire of the moment for immediate expression. The time which was so gladly given to perfect the old dances cannot be spared in our rushing workaday world of the present; so in an intense desire to translate in motion that yearning for expression which is somewhere within each one of us, the strange rush of present-day ballroom dancing has achieved its popularity. It is a kind of reaction perhaps from the rigid formality of the Victorian and Edwardian eras, and indeed from the whole of the artificiality and restrained conditions under which modern life goes on. I verily believe that many of us would develop either into automatons or nerve-wrecks unless there were some outlet for this kind of emotion—for our finer artistic instincts—even if that outlet be only jazz.'

As for the 'old dances' of the ballroom, Pavlova quite enjoyed them, and even sometimes performed them. In Manchester, in 1927 she found a demonstration by Victor Sylvester and his wife 'really beautiful'. Edward Kurylo has recorded dancing a waltz and a polka with her in Bristol, and also acting as a judge with her at a ballroom dancing contest, in aid of Russian charities, in New York in 1916. Mr Kurylo's verdict on her judging was that she very quickly learnt to grasp the good points in ballroom dancing, while his opinion of her dancing the waltz was: 'If she was the queen of ballet dancing, she could easily be the queen of ballroom too.'

CHAPTER SIX

Prima Ballerina Assoluta

THERE is no doubt that Pavlova *was* the queen of ballet, for choreographers who worked with her, members of her company, experienced critics, and virtually everyone who watched her dance. Most of the people who remember her say they have never seen anyone to equal her and they still compare every ballerina they see with their memory of her. They may have recaptured something of her style and impact when watching Toumanova or Markova or Fonteyn but for them Pavlova remains unique. Occasionally some people criticize aspects of her technique, or accuse her of being unmusical, or make superior judgements about her artistic taste. It has even been said that she would not now be considered great, because technical and artistic standards today are allegedly much higher. Every artist, however great, can be criticized and some people seem to enjoy nothing more than denigrating those who are universally accepted as being the leaders of their profession. Nijinsky also had his detractors, just as in our own day there are always some voices ready to tell us about Fonteyn's lack of elevation and weak feet or Nureyev's heavy landings and lack of perfect classical style. In the same way there were those who were so conscious of Maria Callas's occasional sour notes that they could not see why she was the world's most successful prima donna and there were others who found Lord Olivier's acting exaggerated and self-conscious. No artist can appeal to absolutely everybody, and every artist, being human, must have faults. It is also true that standards of taste and styles of performance change from generation to generation so that the acting of Henry Irving would probably seem absurdly 'hammy' today. On the other hand an artist is obviously the child of his or her time; the sort of performance Irving would give if he were alive today is not the sort he actually gave a century ago. Pavlova's repertory and style would equally obviously have been different today.

Nevertheless I believe that Pavlova's performances, exactly as she gave them, would still strike us as great if we could see them now. This opinion is partly based on the descriptions and views of those who did see her. I doubt if anyone with as much stage personality as Pavlova could ever fail to hold an audience, whatever the fashions and tastes of the period. My opinion is also based to some extent on the fragments of films which survive; even though these are primitive and badly lit, and even though the camera speeds rarely give an exact indication of Pavlova's dancing, there are still moments of magic, moments when one is aware of genius.

We have already noted the expressiveness of her body and the softness of her arms in the film records of *The Dying Swan* and the way she conveyed girlish excitement in the simple movements of getting up from a couch and taking off her cloak at the beginning of *Christmas*. There is a *Caucasian Dance* which ends with a long pose, in which Pavlova held out her dress and then did a charming flourish with her hands. In *Fairy Doll* we can see her mischievous yet highly attractive facial expression, her very delicate hand and finger movements, and her beautiful bodily control and poise. In *Californian Poppy* we see her light jump and her very graceful quick little foot and arm movements and we glimpse her charming manner with a fan in a bit of *Rondino*. Similarly in *Dragonfly* we can again admire both her sinuous outstretched arms and her very light, high-speed movements. In extracts from *Don Quixote* we see why people say that they scarcely noticed Pavlova's technique; there are a number of rapid turns but we are so bewitched by her face and general bearing that we do not notice what she actually does with her feet. One dancer described this extraordinary knack of Pavlova's by saying 'she used to emote her turns'. There are awkward moments too; for example in *Danse Grecque* an unfortunate camera-angle results in us seeing rather too much bony knee sticking out. Pavlova herself was very critical of these films and did not wish them to be shown publicly, though she felt she could learn a great deal from watching them. She once remarked that the camera could not even photograph her dress properly, let alone her.

One of the most remarkable bits of dancing in all the Pavlova films comes at the beginning of *The Dumb Girl of Portici*, a ninety-minute silent film directed by Lois Weber in Hollywood in 1915. (It was claimed by Universal at that time to be the most expensive film ever made, costing $250,000 of which Pavlova was supposed to have received $50,000.) It is not a dancing film; instead it represents Pavlova's only attempt at straight acting. But there is a prologue, to remind the audience that the star of the film is the famous ballerina. In this she *bourrées* or runs across the stage on her points and then jumps in the air landing in a perfectly poised and balanced arabesque which is held for what seems a remarkably long space of time. Whether or not this balance is unnaturally prolonged by the camera it is certainly an outstanding piece of dancing. Levinson said that when he remembered Pavlova he preferred to remember her balancing in arabesque; he thought the arabesque was the very foundation of her being.

The Dumb Girl of Portici is generally dismissed, mainly by people who have never seen it, as old-fashioned rubbish. There are very few copies available so it is scarcely ever shown, even in film clubs specializing in old films. When I saw it I was struck by how well-made it is, and it seemed to me to be more interesting and gripping than many old films which are constantly revived. It is a screen adaption of the libretto by Scribe and Delavigne for Auber's opera *La Muette de Portici* which was better known as *Masaniello*. Although this opera is hardly ever staged nowadays, it was once regarded as unusually full of emotion and interesting characterization. The complicated plot is concerned with a popular uprising against a Spanish viceroy in seventeenth-century Italy. The revolt is led by Masaniello, partly protesting against the way the people are treated like cattle and partly trying to avenge his sister Fenella, who had been seduced and abandoned by the viceroy's son Alphonso. Even in the opera the role of Fenella is a dumb one, taken by a ballerina; in the film, of course, all parts are silent. Pavlova as Fenella has a charming smile and a slightly coquettish manner, with a humorous, mocking way of bowing to the aristocracy. When she receives a miniature of Alphonso, whom she believes really loves her, delight and gaiety are clearly shown in her face and gestures. She eagerly rushes out into the street, only to be abducted and flung into prison. She escapes by a rope of sheets, with terror and excitement on her face, and rushes to the place where Alphonso is marrying another girl. The scene when Fenella discovers she is being betrayed is strangely reminiscent of the end of the first act of *Giselle*. In something very much like Giselle's 'mad scene', Pavlova's gestures and facial expressions naturally look exaggerated in close-up before the camera.

But Fenella still loves Alphonso and at the end of the film she is stabbed by Masaniello while trying to shield him. Masaniello then stabs himself and Fenella dies in his arms. Finally Fenella is seen dancing among the clouds—'her spirit lives on'.

The film includes some very realistic crowd scenes for the revolutionary mob as they burst in and break up the viceroy's palace, and Masaniello is a moderate revolutionary leader who says 'liberty not licence' to his followers. There are also scenes of violence which would probably appeal to the cinema public today. Pavlova's performance, despite her total inexperience in straight acting either in the legitimate theatre or in the cinema, is for the most part sincere and moving. I cannot help wondering if she had Tsarist oppression in her native Russia in mind when she made the film.

But however interesting and impressive Pavlova's few screen appearances may be, they can only give us a very partial view of her stage personality, her dramatic range and her dancing style. Even today, with advanced techniques of make-up, photography and sound-recording, the cinema rarely if ever does justice to ballet. Far more reliable evidence about the exact nature of Pavlova's dancing is provided by the detailed descriptions written at the time, and by the subsequent memories of those who saw her.

One thing about which they all agree is the tremendous impact of her stage personality. Early in her career, her first great choreographer, Marius Petipa, said: 'There is one of our dancers who has all the feeling of Duncan and all the techniques of Kshessinskaya. You know who I mean—Anna Pavlova.' Her other great choreographer, Michel Fokine, said: 'It takes a genius to be gay, really gay. When I think of Pavlova it is not the classics, nor the sad wistful evocations of ephemeral things, unique as they were, that I would give as examples of her genius, but *Christmas*. I cannot think of any other dancer who could even make it tolerable, let alone create something that was full of gaiety, the happiest thing ever seen in a theatre.' The French critic J. L. Vaudoyer said: 'Pavlova means to the dance what a Racine is to poetry, a Poussin to painting a Gluck to music.' And the famous teacher and ballet-master Enrico Cecchetti said: 'I can teach everything connected with dancing, but Pavlova has that which can be taught only by God.'

Cyril Beaumont told me that Pavlova had the special gift of attracting attention the moment she came on the stage: 'you did not know how she got there, but suddenly she was there. And you always wanted to see more of her.' A critic in *The Times* made the same point: 'When one sees Mme Pavlova dance, one's greed for more and more easily overcomes one's consideration. It is hard to remember that Mme Pavlova is, after all, a mortal being.' Sir Robert Helpmann told me that the only other artists who have ever had the same electrifying effect on him are Maria Callas and Rudolf Nureyev. Maestro Celli compared the effect of her performances to those of Duse or Caruso: 'the rest of your life was transformed by the experience—it became part of you.' Agnes de Mille, though very critical of Pavlova's choreography and technique, said that 'in her person she was the quintessence of theatrical excitement'. Once Miss de Mille had seen Pavlova dance, 'I had witnessed the power of beauty . . . I was as clearly marked as though she had looked me in the face and called my name.'

Pavlova herself was fully conscious of the effect her personality had on an audience and of the comparisons which could be made between her art and those of actors and painters. When asked where the secret of her success was to be found, she once answered: 'I presume in the sincerity of my art.' And she added: 'I try to express by dancing what the composer puts into his music, what the painter expresses with his colours and brushes, the actor with the spoken word. I try to express them with my body and my spirit, that most universal of all languages.' Dandré wrote: 'She was so light in her dances, so ethereal, so spiritualized, so chaste, that one felt like going on one's knees before her. The feeling of ethereality that emanated from her reached the spectators as if wafted across the land of dreams . . . Even in moments of the greatest technical difficulty no effort or strain was ever visible. She danced in a whisper, if one may use the expression, gliding imperceptibly along the stage.'

This spirituality of Pavlova's dancing is a recurring theme in writing and reminiscences about her. Levinson said that when she danced an extract from Gluck's *Orfeo* she moved as if she was in prayer and that in the second act of *Giselle*, gliding across the stage with a white lily in her hand, it was 'as if an angel had come to announce the birth of a Messiah'. He quoted a priest in Los Angeles as saying that Pavlova was 'worthy to dance before the altar'. And he added that she

'did not quite belong to this world and certainly not to
this age. One recalls the feeling that one had, on seeing her
dance, as of something not of the same stuff as our era, old-
fashioned if you like; or, one might say, not of "our day".
This had to do with her quality of soul, and also with the
visible part of her, charged with spirituality to the utmost.
In a world more and more devoid of mystery, some of her
gestures bordered on the supernatural. She was as much
out of her element in our modern cities as would have been
a péri or any other legendary figure kneaded together out
of reality and the stuff of dreams.'

Part of this effect was doubtless achieved by Pavlova's
careful mental preparation for the roles she danced and
by her total involvement in them. She sank herself into her
roles before going on the stage, and danced in a kind of
trance; she was often carried away on stage, her dancing
reflecting her moods. In *Giselle* she got so involved in the
action that she often scratched the throat of the dancer
miming Berthe, Giselle's mother, and sometimes almost
strangled one of the peasant girls, in Giselle's fury and
anguish at discovering Albrecht's deception. After the
curtain fell on the first act there was often a considerable
pause before she could get up from the stage, where she
had 'died'. Walford Hyden recorded that when some enthusiastic Russian cossacks burst on to the stage in Glasgow
while she was dancing, it was not so much their presence
that upset her but the shock when they actually spoke,
shattering the silence of the world in which she lived on
stage. Her dancers knew better than to speak to her during
a performance—she was 'carried away', Leon Kellaway said,
'as if she was not on this earth'.

To some extent Pavlova's spirituality and total involvement with her roles was specifically Russian. Many of the
great ballerinas of the Imperial Russian Ballet had a similar
quality and I am often told by those who remember them
that it is this spirituality which our dancers, however gifted
technically, totally lack today. It may have been the result

of the segregated, strictly old-fashioned upbringing of the Imperial Ballet School; it may have been the Russian soul.

Pavlova thought it was a specifically Russian characteristic to immerse oneself completely in one's stage work. In one of her articles in the *Strand Magazine* she wrote: 'When dancing, a Slav can allow no other thought than the perfect translation of the movements he performs . . . it is because he can surrender himself so completely to his art that the Slav exhibits it so beautifully.' And in an interview in an earlier issue of the same magazine, she said that English 'calmness, reserve and self-control, all much admired qualities in everyday and home life, form rather a hindrance to the stage artiste, whose personality must be given away with both hands. You should be allowed to cry when you are sad and be exuberant in your joy when you feel happy, and not make secrets of either emotion. The artiste can have no secrets. On the stage we must be able to use our personalities to indicate every kind of emotion to the audience. It is clear—is it not?—that we can only learn to do this successfully if off the stage we let ourselves go all the time, if we sob when we are miserable and laugh when we are glad.'

In addition to these Slav characteristics, there was something about Pavlova's face which had a hypnotic effect on her audiences. She was not beautiful, in any conventional sense, but she became beautiful as she danced. Sir Frederick Ashton said that the first time he saw her come on the stage, when he was a young boy, he thought 'how ugly' but by the time she had finished *Fairy Doll* he thought 'how beautiful'. Men who went to see her simply hoping for a bit of glamour were sometimes disappointed. Pavlova was occasionally hurt by reviews saying she lacked sex-appeal. In those days the ideal of beauty was rather buxom while she was exceptionally thin. In an interview in the *Berliner Zeitung* as early as 1909 she said that women often liked her better than men. 'Men like ballerinas who are beautiful and more "belle femme"', she said. 'Women say "Look how thin and tender she is.

She probably has a good heart and is very nice." I live with my heart on the stage and express the most tender feelings of a woman, and her sufferings. Women have more understanding for these nuances.' (Incidentally, at that time, twenty-one years before death stopped her dancing, Pavlova thought she would only be able to dance for ten more years at the most.)

Perhaps her eyes were the most hypnotic and fascinating features of her face, as they are of Dame Margot Fonteyn's. When Sidney Dark interviewed Pavlova for the *Strand Magazine* in 1924 he wrote: 'When you talk to her, you only notice her eyes. They intrigue, they excite, they fascinate. You feel that they hide a wilderness of wonderful secrets. They are the eyes of a dreamer, a poet, an artiste.' The distinguished British music critic Ernest Newman found her whole face intriguing. Writing in the *Birmingham Post*, he said: 'Pavlova's face, like the rest of her, is an enigma that she probably does not comprehend herself. Who can say whether that fascinating but baffling expression comes from extreme simplicity or extreme subtlety of soul? One can think of nothing quite so eloquent yet so elusive and indefinable since the smile of the Mona Lisa.' Geraldine Spencer described her face as 'ageless', the face of 'a being apart, an immortal'. More precisely, Cyril Beaumont described Pavlova's face as 'pale and oval, her forehead high, her hair dark and drawn close to her head; her nose was slightly aquiline, her cheekbones high, her eyes large and the colour of dark brown cherries. Her head was beautifully poised on a swan-like neck, her expression was part-elfin, part-mischievous, part-imperious, and it could be as changeable as the very face of nature.' Continuing his physical description he wrote: 'Her fingers tended to be thick, but when she danced she managed them so skilfully that the hands seemed delicate and the fingers tapering.'

Pavlova was considered slightly tall for a ballerina in her own time, when most Russian ballerinas were extremely petite. She was about 5 ft. 4 in., the same height as Dame

Margot Fonteyn. Pavlova had narrow ankles and an exceptionally high instep, which made her perfection on her points all the more remarkable. (It is rare for a dancer with a big instep to be correctly vertical on her points). Moreover Dandré said that her toes were of very different lengths so that the big toes had to bear nearly all her weight when she was on her points. Many of her dancers suspected that she treated her ballet shoes in some special way to make pointwork easier, but they never discovered her secret, if she had one. Certainly her shoes were not heavily blocked in the modern manner, which often makes point dancing sound like tap dancing. On the contrary her shoes were very soft. She took immense trouble over them, removing the sole and putting in her own piece of cardboard, and strengthening the ribbons with tape in case they snapped. Pavlova had enormous difficulty in finding comfortable shoes, both for dancing and for ordinary use. She bought dozens of pairs, and often discarded them immediately; nearly all her ballet shoes were specially supplied by a shoemaker in Milan but even these often failed to suit her. Pavlova's discarded shoes kept the other girls in her company in fairly constant supply.

The short answer to those who criticize Pavlova's technique is that she would never have become a prima ballerina of the Maryinsky Theatre without a remarkable technique. It is true that her legs and feet were not quite as well or naturally turned out as those of some dancers, and at the beginning and end of her career she often had difficulty in doing turns on the stage when she was not supported by a partner. She liked her partner to help her around. On her best form, however, she could do marvellous turns. Once in class, after reprimanding a girl for practising *fouettés*, which she regarded as a circus stunt, Pavlova showed how they should be done. Algeranoff remembered a performance of *Fairy Doll* when she suddenly did nineteen or twenty extra 'finger' pirouettes while the conductor had to keep the music going. Similarly, Pavlova is often described as a 'terre à terre' dancer, one who could not jump very high. This was only true towards the end of her career; at the beginning she was famous for her lightness and her jump. (Like most ballerinas, Pavlova was probably at her peak, technically, in her late thirties and early forties; Novikoff was struck by the improvement in her technique when he rejoined her after the first world war.) Svetlov said that, beside her, other dancers seemed 'terre à terre'. No other dancer could do complex pirouettes with such neatness and precision, nor equal the delicacy of her 'pizzicato' footwork and the strength of her steel-like points. Her balance, he said, lasted beyond the limits of what seemed possible or imaginable and yet it was all done easily, naturally, without any apparent effort. Svetlov claimed that Pavlova even invented new steps, which he called 'les trilles de jambes et les fermatas sur les pointes' and which he thought were remarkably beautiful. He noted that some of her poses and plastic gestures were new and unexpected, not at all those of a conventional classical dancer.

Svetlov might be suspected of partiality in his enthusiasm, but numerous dancers who worked with Pavlova and who later became ballet teachers confirm his praise of her technique. Leon Kellaway, of the Australian Ballet School, said her strength was in the pelvis and the trunk of her body, enabling her to achieve incredible balances. Like Svetlov, he remembered the way she held arabesques; in *Amarilla* she held one for a long time and then launched into a series of pirouettes. In *Snowflakes* she ran on and held a balance indefinitely while the music was slowed down to wait for her. Mme Cléo Nordi, a London teacher, confirmed that Pavlova was not a 'terre à terre' dancer, but light and aerial. She considered that Pavlova was fundamentally a product of the Legat method, which stressed quick thinking and movement and the interesting combination of different steps. Cecchetti's more formal style was superimposed on this. The Legat system encouraged spontaneity and made dancers think for themselves; the Cecchetti system was more rigidly prescribed, with dancers tending to repeat the same exercises and steps every day.

Rozella Frey, a Los Angeles teacher, considered Pavlova a great technician. She thought it was Pavlova's deep plié (bending of the knees) which made her jump so well. On stage, she said, Pavlova was like a piece of steel; however soft her arms might be, her centre was always firm and strong. In addition she instinctively felt the music—'her feet heard it'. Miss Frey stressed that although Pavlova had this fine technique, she never threw it at the audience, so that spectators were almost unaware of it. Mme Xenia Borovansky, a teacher in Melbourne, Australia, made the same point: Pavlova detested dancers who used their bodies like rigid machines and always insisted that the body must look relaxed and supple.

Nevertheless Pavlova did have technical tricks of her own which invariably won a round of applause. Svetlov's 'trilles' and 'fermatas' are probably something like what Sir Frederick Ashton had in mind when he recalled the way she could do very fast turns and suddenly stop absolutely still in an arabesque, not wobbling or moving at all, as most dancers would have done. Ashton and Mary Skeaping both told me of the way Pavlova travelled backwards across the stage at great speed in *Amarilla*, as if skating on ice, while bending down in an 'arabesque penché' and shaking a tambourine almost at ground-level. This was extremely difficult to do and looked very exciting.

One of the most controversial aspects of Pavlova's dancing was her use of music. Conductors were expected to watch her and adjust their tempi to suit her balances and spins, and to fit the speed she felt appropriate to her dancing. This often led to disputes, especially with Walford Hyden who took a rigid, purist view of how music should be played. Pavlova's attitude was that the music existed as an accompaniment to her art, not that she existed to fit some conductor's conception of the music. This attitude was fully in accordance with the traditional practice of the Imperial

Russian Ballet. Riccardo Drigo, the composer and conductor at the Maryinsky during most of Petipa's reign, was regarded as a first-class ballet conductor. He not only conducted performances but also played the piano at rehearsals; he knew all the repertoire from memory and he understood the variations in speed required by different dancers. When conducting, he was always ready to adjust his tempi, according to whether a dancer felt weak or strong that night. Pavlova's first public performances were conducted by Drigo, and this was the sort of conducting she always demanded. She got it for most of her career from her regular musical director, Theodore Stier. As she did not use symphonic music, but mainly light salon pieces specifically arranged for ballet, she was surely justified in expecting the music to be adjusted to fit her needs.

Kathleen Crofton, a teacher in Buffalo, New York, argued that Pavlova was so musical that she instinctively knew how long she could hold a balance to a particular section of music without distorting it. Conductors like Walford Hyden were unmusical, she said, because they were so rigid. This view is supported by a Russian critic, Yuri Belyaev, who said: 'She was so extremely musical that she could appreciate the emotional content of a piece and could treat it freely in her own way without considering the composer's own original idea. She shortened music or changed its tempo because she saw and felt everything through her own emotions. And it was this gift which made her a great dancer.' Svetlov remarked on her sense of rhythm and on the way she instinctively danced to the musical accent. Serge Lifar, on the other hand, said: 'She was a dancer of genius, but an inadequate interpreter of the musical image', a judgement which would carry greater weight if it came from a choreographer who was more obviously sensitive to music in his own work.

Lifar may have been jaundiced about Pavlova because various efforts he made to dance with her came to nothing. He did actually rehearse with her once in preparation for a gala in memory of Diaghilev at the Paris Opéra, but Pavlova later withdrew from the performance. Lifar said that when he danced with her he found her too 'turned-in'; there is no record of how she found him. But Pavlova's partners obviously had to be willing to fit in with her ideas, rather than to assert their own. In a film about Pavlova made for National Educational Television in the United States in 1967, Aubrey Hitchens said: 'To partner her was extremely difficult—she concealed all preparations for lifts and pirouettes. One had to learn when she was going to take off for a lift by a most subtle movement from her heel. She would be running and then up, with no visible preparation. Split-second timing was needed. She looked frail but her body was like steel.' Apart from the problem of timing, Pavlova was not difficult to lift, as she was light and helped herself up. André Olivéroff wrote: 'I was scarcely conscious at all of her weight; her elevation seemed to continue after she had come into position, held up in the air by my hands. Some ballerinas, when you hold them like that, seem to be made of stone, though their weight on the scales be actually less than was Madame's. But in some way Madame helped you to support her—she seemed always to be reaching up, giving you the illusion that she was very much lighter than she really was, by a sort of telepathy, I always believed. You almost felt she might fly away on the wind at any moment, like a piece of swan's down. You never, even if you were fagged, dreaded the moment when you had to lift her—a fact worth mentioning, since it certainly counted in the resulting theatrical effect.'

Edward J. Kurylo agreed with this. He wrote: 'I partnered Pavlova once on the stage. It was in England in 1912, when her partner, Novikoff, became ill. Then I could understand why she was so different from all other dancers. First of all, she never depended on her partner's support while she was dancing. She pirouetted without assistance, and when the moment came for her to be picked up in the air she helped so much (and, mind you, she was as light as a feather) that

her partner did not tire himself for his own solo to come.'
No doubt Pavlova made a particular effort to help when her
partner was new and inexperienced; on other occasions she
certainly required 'assistance' with her pirouettes and she
sometimes faced her partners with challenging situations
caused by her sudden improvisations. One of her complaints
against Pierre Vladimirov, her last regular partner, was that
he did not watch her sufficiently and was not always where
she needed him on the stage.

Whatever argument there might be about Pavlova's use
of music and her 'turn-out', there was none about her
'line' and her use of her arms. 'Line' is the ability of a dancer
to move and stand in such a way that the whole body—
head, torso, arms and legs—always forms a harmonious and
attractive pattern. It is partly a matter of good physical
proportions, partly a matter of instinct, and partly a matter
of training. Pavlova was noted for her natural 'line' from
the moment she first went to ballet school and it remained
with her always, on and off stage. And her 'port de bras', the
use of her arms, was always admired. Maestro Celli said
the sentiment expressed by her arms and hands was un-
equalled. Her arms contributed at least as much as her
footwork to solos like *The Swan* and *The Dragonfly*.

The role in which Pavlova's dancing technique, acting
ability and unique spirituality were most completely blended
was of course *Giselle*. Even Serge Lifar, with his many criticisms of Pavlova, was lost in praise: 'It was no longer the
dancer Pavlova, it was Giselle eternally dying and eternally
resuscitated, ghostly and imponderable . . . Such was her
dying there on the stage, that one always seemed to be
bidding her a last farewell. It was as though only the merest
film separated life from death, the woman dancer from the
ghost of a vision.'

Writing about Pavlova's dancing in general, Lifar said:
'Her airy lightness seemed to defy the very laws of gravity.
I was shaken through and through, and completely en-
slaved by the simplicity, the ease, the plasticity of her art.

Not one *fouetté*, not one trick of the virtuoso, but loveliness alone. She seemed to glide through the air without making the least effort, as though it were some divine Mozartian gift, which left her free to add nothing at all. In Anna Pavlova I saw not the dancer, but the very *genius* of the dance, as I prostrated myself before that divine manifestation. For the first moments I had no use for my reason; I could not, and dared not see any fault or imperfection. I was gazing at some divine revelation, I was no longer on this earth. All through the performance I felt either away up in the clouds or down on the earth. Now a divine gesture, or classical "pose" would make me tremble in reverent awe, than again a hint of unnecessary skittishness would appear in her miming, a taint of something akin to "stunting", to cheapness even, and then my enthusiasm would suffer a severe blow.'

A critic in *The Times* responded to her *Giselle* in a similar way: 'She is tragedy itself. There is a wild intensity about her miming in the scene of her madness and death which is at once heartrending and subduing. Equally marvellous in its way is her dancing in the graveyard episode, which is the dancing not of gross mortal clay but of an incorporeal spirit.'

Many of Pavlova's dancers have recalled how moved they were by her *Giselle*, even in rehearsals, and how tense the atmosphere used to be as she got into the necessary mood before a performance. They really believed in her madness, they often cried at her 'death', and they were awed and overcome when she rose from the grave. Pavlova evidently succeeded in carrying out her own advice to dancers: '*Be*, don't just dance, or act, simply *be*.' Winifred Edwards considered that Pavlova's Giselle was one of the best pieces of acting she had even seen. Sol Hurok said that nobody else actually *was* Giselle as Pavlova was: 'She lived through it each time.'

But Pavlova's identification with all her roles, however minor, tended to be equally complete. Just as she *was* Giselle she *was* the Swan or the Dragonfly. Many of her solos would have seemed unbearably trite and over-sentimental but for the sincerity and conviction she brought to them.

This applied both to tragedy and to comedy, to her 'spiritual' roles and her coquettish ones. Most ballerinas are essentially tragédiennes, or soubrettes; very few are sufficiently versatile to be equally at home in either style. Pavlova was. She also had the rare ability, as Fonteyn had later, of almost unconsciously adopting the poses and movements of a period as she put on the appropriate costume. Svetlov said that it was only necessary for her to be photographed in a dress of 1830 for the result to look like an authentic early nineteenth-century picture.

Stage costumes were very important to Pavlova, being an essential part of her interpretation of a role. She often designed her own costumes, as for *The Dragonfly* and *Californian Poppy*, and she did not allow members of her company to adapt the costumes originally designed for their roles. Pavlova's bodices were made at home by her faithful Manya, who was with her for eighteen years, and then sent to Paris if necessary for additional decorations to be sewn on. Her head-dresses were also made at home to ensure that they were light and firmly fitting. Several thousand yards of tarlatan were imported every year from the United States for her ballet skirts; she insisted that the material should not be too soft, like a rag, nor too firm, standing out stiffly. *The Swan* costume was never worn more than twice without the skirt of the tutu being renewed. Pavlova could not identify herself with her various roles unless she knew that the costumes were exactly right.

In other words Pavlova's identification with characters and periods was not a purely instinctive thing, but a conscious combination of instinct and careful preparation, physical and mental. She forced herself to perform almost equally well whether or not she was in the mood and in good health. Obviously she could not always rely on spontaneous inspiration when she had to dance eight or nine performances a week, frequently doing ten different dances in each programme, involving four changes of costume, make-up, style and mood. The appearance of inspiration came from total dedication and extreme professionalism, allied with her almost childlike ability to sink into a role at will. Naturally Pavlova was surrounded by sycophants and fans, and found it difficult to get honest, informed criticism. She certainly wanted it. Arnold Haskell recounted how furious she was once, at Ivy House, when she got excessive applause after dancing *The Dying Swan*. 'How dare they applaud like that?' she asked. 'I know I danced badly. It is no compliment to an artist, I shall lose all my standards if people aren't more discriminating.' Once in Holland Pavlova instructed a young dancer who was off with an injury to watch *La Fille Mal Gardée*, and make frank comments afterwards. When the girl nervously made a few mild criticisms, Pavlova said: 'Ah, you think I am bad. Never before has someone told me I am bad. Everybody tells me, Madam you are wonderful, you are marvellous. I know this is not true because sometimes I don't feel so good and I know I don't dance so well.' And she gave the girl a chocolate and a kiss.

There are countless stories about Pavlova dancing when she did not 'feel so good'. In St. Louis, Missouri, she hurt her left ankle during a rehearsal and news of the injury reached the newspapers. When reporters asked her which ankle was injured she said it was her right one. 'You see', she explained to her dancers afterwards, 'now they will watch the right ankle during the performance, and nothing will seem amiss.' When she had a cold she did an extra class 'to sweat it out'; when she had a bad sore throat she had injections to enable her to carry on. She once danced *Giselle* with such a high temperature that she fainted three times; on another occasion she fainted after doing *The Dying Swan*. According to André Olivéroff her audiences suspected nothing.

Once Pavlova was in such a depressed mood, for some

reason, that she could not bring herself to dance her celebrated *Gavotte*. She stayed in her dressing-room sobbing, while the music played, but then she danced some other items later in the programme instead. She never cancelled a performance because of any indisposition or temperament. During the last years of her life she suffered from a chronic knee injury which sometimes caused her severe pain. She would not consider an operation, which would have put an end to her dancing. When she asked a doctor in South Africa what she should do and he advised rest for three weeks, she answered: 'I know that, but what must I do?' As far as she was concerned, rest was not a possibility she could even consider. She would tell her dancers: 'You must not be tired—the audience has a right to be tired because they have been working all day at jobs they don't like, but we are artists and have to help them get over their fatigue.' Sometimes she would even say, crudely, that she could no more allow herself to be tired than she could make a mess in the corner, instead of going to the toilet. In 1929 in Australia, when she was approaching fifty and her young company were all exhausted after days of rehearsals and matinées, a journalist asked her if she was tired. 'Tired?' she replied, 'No, that is not for me.'

This determination and will-power were not things which Pavlova developed to meet the economic exigencies of her world tours. They were characteristic of her throughout her career. Even in her early days, in Russia, she had insisted on dancing *Giselle* when she had flu, and she had signed a document releasing the management of the Maryinsky Theatre from any responsibility for the effect on her health. Self-discipline, spirituality, simplicity and child-like naiveté were all part of her dancing, and like her dancing, they were also all extensions of her personality.

CHAPTER SEVEN

Lonely Child

PEOPLE who associate Pavlova only with *The Dying Swan* and *Giselle*, tend to think of her as rather a dull sort of person, totally dedicated to the dance, vaguely soulful and spiritual, but without any private life and without very much sparkle to her personality. Those who remember also her lively and coquettish dances suspect that she must have had another side to her personality as well. But to nearly everyone, including those who worked with her and knew her for many years, she remains enigmatic. It was not for nothing that her dancers referred to her, behind her back, as 'X'. Ernest Newman's analogy with the Mona Lisa is remarkably apt, and the same analogy was drawn by Hubert Stowitts who said that if Da Vinci had painted Pavlova, the world would never have given the Mona Lisa its fame.

There are many mysteries about Pavlova, quite apart from the initial uncertainty about her parentage. What drove her to go on dancing, in trying and tiring conditions all round the world, when she could well have afforded to rest on her reputation or restrict her appearances to the world's leading opera-houses? What exactly was the nature of her relationship with Victor Dandré? Was she really religious? Was she happy in her work and in her life?

In her own brief memoir, Pavlova wrote: 'In my opinion, a true artist must devote herself wholly to her art. She has no right to lead the life that most women long for ... What exactly is success? For me it is to be found not in applause, but in the satisfaction of feeling that one is realizing one's ideal. When, a small child, I was rambling over there by the fir trees, I thought that success spelled happiness. I was wrong. Happiness is like a butterfly which appears and delights us for one brief moment, but soon flits away.' The butterfly analogy is of course very typical of Pavlova, as she was constantly thinking of and talking to animals, birds and insects. This passage expresses very clearly her belief in the dedicated mission of the artist as well as hinting at her failure to find complete satisfaction in her life. She certainly had a missionary zeal about her dancing. She often said things like 'I want to dance for everyone in the world', or 'I do not dance for the critics but for this one who is poor, or this one who is sick, or worried, or has someone sick at home'. One of her motives in forcing herself to go on dancing, year in year out, was simply this missionary zeal, the feeling that she had a duty to give her art to the whole world. She also developed a loyalty to her company, which depended on her for its existence. And above all she had a psychological need to dance, because dancing was her life.

Of course Pavlova had other interests. She painted and made little sculptures; although she had no formal training as an artist, some of her busts of herself dancing, moulded in bronze or porcelain, are considered to capture the style and mood of her dancing rather well. Sometimes she would ask a dancer to pose in various positions for her in her room without indicating that she was using her as a model. She was an indefatigable visitor to art galleries and museums: Florence was one of her favourite places, and she also liked Venice and Siena. Her favourite Italian sculptors were Michelangelo and Donatello, her preferred painters were Da Vinci, Botticelli and Sodoma. She was romantic in her choice of composers and writers too; she told Philip Richardson, the founder of the *Dancing Times*, that her favourite western composers were Mendelssohn and Auber, her poet was Alfred de Musset and her novelist was Sir Walter Scott. In an interview published in the United States on her first visit there, in 1910, her favourite novelist was stated to be Turgenev and her favourite contemporary writer, Andreyev.

Perhaps she had not yet discovered many Western writers at that time; certainly she was still very naive about the western world. In the same interview she remarked that the Holy Synod of the Russian Orthodox Church had forbidden the production of Andreyev's play *Anathema*, although it had already been seen by hundreds of people in Russia. She asked if this meant it could not be performed in the United States, and when the interviewer asked her if she thought that Russian laws prevailed in America, she answered: 'Don't they?'

Pavlova always retained a special love for Russia and everything Russian, as do most Russians in exile. Throughout her life she thought of herself and her art as essentially Russian. When explaining in the *Strand Magazine* why Slavs make the best dancers, she wrote: 'All Russians are ardent lovers of music and poetry . . . There is always to be found a close relationship between the excellence of a nation's dancing and the excellence of its arts, and an inherent love of these things probably helps us to perfection. We Russians dance because to us dancing is a true ideal, one perfect in itself. Possibly this is an outcome of the fact that Russia is the home of folk-dancing and that for centuries we have immortalized in action stories those beautiful legends of folk-lore which other nations have confined to books.'

But Pavlova was critical of state and church censorship in Russia and aware of the poverty and oppression of the people under the Tsars. She had some initial sympathy with the aims of the Russian Revolution. Occasionally she talked wistfully of returning to Russia and of the progress allegedly being made under the Soviet regime, but this sort of talk made Dandré turn pale; he never shared any of her more revolutionary sympathies, either in ballet or in politics. Later even Pavlova's enthusiasm for the Soviet experiment evaporated, especially when money she tried to send to artists in Russia was rejected as tainted by capitalism. However she shared the traditional Russian suspicion of western commercialism, disliking the fact that she and her art had

to be advertised and the way in which her name was sometimes used to promote various beauty products. She burst
into tears the first time she saw herself advertised on top of
a London bus. And she hated the necessity to adjust her art
and her repertoire to meet box-office requirements. As late
as 1926 she told the *Sydney Morning Herald* that 'in Russian art,
they do not measure the results by the box-office receipts',
a comment which applied equally to Russia under the
Tsars and under the Soviets. Despite her vague left-wing
sympathies, however, Pavlova also had an innate respect
for royalty; Fokine said that she rejected his idea for a
Coq d'Or ballet in 1912 because she did not approve of the
implied satire on central European monarchs.

Despite her lasting nostalgia for Russia, Pavlova was very
happy in her English home, Ivy House, where she relaxed
with her books, animals, birds and flowers. It had once been
the home of Turner, the landscape painter, and it was
almost a country house. It was certainly as near to the
country as she wanted to live—she did not fancy a primitive

A Christmas card sent out by Pavlova
(Mander-Mitchenson Theatre Collection)

rural life—and perhaps it reminded her a little of her childhood at the *dacha* in Ligovo. There were two verandahs over-
looking the garden, with its miniature 'swan lake'. In
addition to her swans, she had a little aviary and she personally supervised the building of a pigeon house on the
roof. There were flamingoes and a peacock on the lawn and
she had a variety of dogs and cats, as well as constantly
bringing exotic birds and other pets back from her foreign
tours. She once bought a hundred and twenty birds in
Australia to take back to England by sea. Sometimes she
even brought flowers from abroad and tried to replant them,
especially if they were the sort of wild flowers which reminded her of Russia, like some she found in the Dolomites.
Most of these transplant operations were unsuccessful,
though she did succeed in growing boronia, brought back
from Australia.

Pavlova loved lying in a hammock, watching the birds
taking a bath, having a garden tea with her friends, or talking
to her swans. She trained the swans to be remarkably tame;
they even posed with her for photographs. In the film called
Immortal Swan, compiled by Dandré after her death, we see
her relaxing in the garden of Ivy House, playing with her
dog and arranging flowers, and we actually hear her calling
to her swans, in what is probably the only existing recording
of her voice. She gives a charming warm laugh and then
calls 'come here', come on'. Pavlova was extremely sentimental in her attitude to animals and birds, and even to
plants. She never lost any chance of talking to animals, or
posing for photographs with them; elephants, camels and
sheep were as welcome as swans and dogs. When she went
fishing in Singapore she threw all the fish back in the water
because she could not bear to see them gasping for air,
though she loved eating fish. And she hated to see flowers
tied up in wire or string; after performances all her bouquets
had immediately to be 'freed'.

The hall of Ivy House was big enough for ballet classes
and rehearsals, and there were huge cellars which were used

for storing the company's costumes, wigs and musical scores. In addition to Dandré, her small entourage of permanent servants lived there too, including a Russian chef, Vladimir. Pavlova never lost her taste for Russian delicacies like rye bread, pirozhki (meat and vegetable patties), blinis (pancakes) with sour cream and caviare, meat rissoles and kasha (buckwheat served as a vegetable), and she liked to wash them down with vodka. She did not usually eat a great deal of any one dish but she nibbled at lots of different things. She had no dietetic inhibitions about trying and enjoying a bit of everything; in American cafeterias she often selected enough food to fill two trays, so that she could taste all the various dishes with which she was unfamiliar, and she would eat them in any haphazard order, sometimes starting with the dessert and ending with the soup.

Although Pavlova rehearsed and practised at Ivy House, she regarded it mainly as a place for rest and relaxation between tours. Sorin painted his celebrated portrait of her there in 1922, but according to Sol Hurok she never forgave the artist for making her pose throughout a six-week 'holiday'. But of course even on 'holiday', her friends, thoughts and conversations were never far from the ballet. Olivéroff recounted an incident at a typical Ivy House lunch party, when Pavlova and Novikoff got into an argument about the correct way for him to lift her in *Russian Folk Lore*. Suddenly they both got up from the table to demonstrate, but, perhaps because of post-prandial confusion, Novikoff had no sooner lifted Pavlova high above his head than they both fell flat on the floor. Pavlova was unhurt but Dandré was not amused. Pavlova, according to Olivéroff, 'had the self-conscious air of a child who had been caught unawares at mischief and suddenly remembered to be very proper and good'.

References to Pavlova behaving 'like a child' abound in the various reminiscences of her. And there was indeed something essentially child-like in her personality, in her enthusiasms, her tempers, her naiveté, her impulsiveness, and even in her relationship with Dandré. He was eleven years older than she was, and was very much her protector and manager. Like the other men with whom she had affairs in her early days in Russia, he was doubtless a kind of father-figure, replacing the real father she never knew. Olivéroff remarked that Dandré started as her lover but became her father; he idolized her and she sometimes rebelled against him exactly like an adolescent child. Sometimes she hurled her shoes at him backstage in a rage; at other times she would treat him contemptuously, ordering him about like an important ballerina dealing with an administrative official. He actually left her once, during the 1914–18 war, taking the boat back to London when she was dancing in New York. But the separation did not last long. Arnold Haskell thought that Dandré was always slightly afraid of her; there were weeks on end when Pavlova and Dandré did not speak to each other. But Pavlova could not cope with the cares of the world and the business side of her career without Dandré, and she was doubtless grateful to him for his considerable early help in Russia. Dandré would have been nothing without Pavlova, whom he idolized. Their relationship was based on long association and mutual dependence, though it struck many people as more like a business partnership than a marriage.

There is in fact considerable doubt about whether they were actually married. If they were, the ceremony probably took place near New York in 1914. That is what Dandré said after Pavlova's death and that is what Mme Manya claimed to remember: she said that Pavlova, Dandré, Cecchetti, Clustine and a few others drove out of New York one day and when they came back Pavlova said she had been secretly married. On the other hand, Sol Hurok said definitely that no marriage ever took place, but that in 1925 he announced one for publicity purposes. No record of the wedding has ever been produced and it would have been surprising, though not quite impossible, for it to have taken place

without any publicity at all. It seems probable that in fact
Pavlova and Dandré were never legally married; certainly
they were never married according to the rites of the
Russian Orthodox Church.

If Pavlova had been as religious as is often stated, she
would neither have lived with a man to whom she was not
married nor would she have accepted any form of marriage
but the solemn rites of the Church in which she was brought
up. It is true that she crossed herself frequently, in the
Russian manner, and always did so before going onto the
stage, that she had an ikon by her bed, even when she travelled, and that she sat and prayed before leaving home on a
journey. But these customs were inbred in Russians of her
generation; they did not necessarily indicate any profound
religious conviction nor were they always associated with
regular church-going. Pavlova scarcely ever went to church,
except at important annual ceremonies like Easter, the
biggest event in the Russian Orthodox calendar. When she
did go, she hated to see the church used as a social meeting
place for Russian exiles and she disapproved of political
sermons. She was mystical and slightly superstitious. Cléo
Nordi, who was a member of the Theosophical Society, said
that Pavlova used to love discussing her theosophical beliefs.
Pavlova was interested in such questions as whether genius
was a gift from God, acquired at birth, or something
developed through environment and education; she inclined to the first view. Pavlova's superstitions took many
forms. At a royal command performance in Brunswick in
1914, when she knelt to kiss the Kaiserin's hand she left a
bright lipstick print, which she was sure was an augury of
bloodshed and war. At her final performance at Golders
Green someone sent her a tribute looking rather like a
funeral wreath, which seemed another bad omen. She spent
several hours sitting up with it, illuminated by candles.
And she forgot to make her usual round of farewells to her
pets and her favourite pieces of furniture when she left Ivy
House for what turned out to be the last time in 1930. Maybe

she was psychic rather than religious; when she spent a night alone in the Egyptian desert, in communion with the sphinx and much to the alarm of her friends, she returned in the morning claiming to be uplifted by the experience. Walford Hyden thought she was either divinely protected or remarkably lucky, because of the way she just missed earthquakes, revolutions, and accidents in her travels. If there is such a thing as being accident-prone, she was the opposite.

The truth about Pavlova's religion is that she did not observe the formal teachings or rituals of any church, but that she had a strong sense of the importance of truth and beauty, and an intuitive spiritual sense. In her youth she helped the church to some extent; for example during her first American tours she and her dancers made a new carpet for the altar steps of the Theatre School chapel in St. Petersburg. In later years her charity was directed towards deserving individuals. Pavlova had an instinctive sympathy for the poor and the ill, and a strong natural desire to help them. She sometimes sought out dancers who had long left her company, taking them money and presents if they were sick or in poverty. She sent a generous allowance to her mother in Russia and she also gave one to her former lover, Svetlov, when he was living with Trefilova in Paris. But her favourite charity was the Russian Children's Home in Paris which she set up to look after the many Russian orphans in Paris after the Russian Revolution. She often gave special performances in aid of this Home. Here is the appeal she put in her Covent Garden programmes in 1924:

'During the year 1921, when in Paris, the worst hardships I witnessed were those endured by the little Russian children, some without homes, many actually starving—little refugees of my own land merely pleading for help in a strange country. Something had to be done at once so, at St Cloud, near Paris, I rented for some of them a suitable home, where they now live in happiness and are well cared for. That little band is ever increasing; already it has assumed

proportions beyond my private purse to entirely support.
I am most anxious to continue this work—will you please
help me?'

When Pavlova founded this Home she tried to raise the
money by a series of special performances in Paris, intending
to give three quarters of the proceeds to her new charitable
foundation and one quarter to the orphans of French ex-
servicemen. But one of these performances was held in the
open-air, on what turned out to be a wet day, and lost
money. Pavlova gave the small profit on the venture
entirely to French orphans and launched her Home with
her private funds. It was a pleasant house with a lovely
garden; it started with fifteen Russian girls who were
adopted and given a complete academic and moral education. An appeal for funds sent directly to nearly eight
thousand rich Americans did not win much response,
though a Ford offered to pay the complete cost of educating
one girl. Pavlova also obtained help from the American
'Camp Fire Girls'. Pavlova approved of this organization
similar to the 'Girl Guides' which was intended to train
girls in independence but to protect them from what was
regarded as the permissiveness of the age. She attended
several camps, taking a keen interest in the girls, and was
elected an honorary 'Camp Fire Girl' at a ceremony at
which she had to light a bonfire. The girls gave a thousand
dollars towards her Home. Photographs of Pavlova were
generally sold in aid of the Home but most of the costs
were born out of Pavlova's own pocket. In 1928, when the
French Government imposed a heavy tax on all foreign
property, Pavlova had to sell the house at St Cloud. The
girls were now mostly seventeen or eighteen years old and
the money obtained from the sale was used to help support
them independently. Altogether, forty-five girls passed
through the Home.

Pavlova felt deeply for the suffering of her fellow Russians,
whether at home or abroad. After the Revolution she gave
several charity performances in aid of famine relief and

medical supplies for Russia; in Brussels she staged a special patriotic scena, to Tchaikowsky music, with herself as 'Russia' and another dancer as 'Belgium'. A performance in New York raised $5,000 which was sent to Russia to help students and former students of the theatre schools. But in 1929 the Soviet Government vetoed the distribution of Pavlova's money, saying it was unacceptable to the artists because it came from a tainted capitalist source and must be given to the Red Army instead. Fortunately most of it had already been distributed before this veto. To the end of her days, even though her income had fallen, Pavlova could never refuse a request for aid from any of the destitute Russians she encountered in Paris or Berlin.

But Russians were by no means the only calls on her charity. At the beginning of the first world war she gave a performance in aid of the Red Cross at the Metropolitan, New York, writing a personal message for the appeal leaflet:

'At this tragic moment of our existence, my heart longs to express its sympathy and be of service to suffering humanity, to help the bereft women and children of Europe, and those who are laying down their lives for their country, I can offer nothing but my art. It is a poor thing when such brave deeds are being done, yet if you will all help me I will do my utmost, give the best that is in me to ease the terrible suffering of our brave brothers.'

Pavlova's generous nature and soft heart were so well-known that she was constantly receiving begging letters with various hard-luck stories. Those closest to her did their best to prevent her yielding to every request, which would have involved her being bamboozled as often as not. When in doubt, she preferred to give rather than risk denying help to a deserving case. On one occasion, when her ear-rings were stolen, she refused to report the loss to the police, saying 'Never mind, they probably need those earrings more than I do'. Not that she was indifferent to personal property; she was very upset whenever anything of hers disappeared, and disliked the thought of people coveting each other's belongings. She was scrupulous about the prompt return of any handkerchief or book that might be lent to her; it was not the value of an object that affected her but the fact that it was somebody's personal possession. In fact, as she never carried money and had little head for figures, she could easily appear either mean or absurdly erratic in money matters. In Berlin in 1909 she left some jewels, said to be worth a hundred thousand marks, in a taxi on the way to her hotel from the theatre. The driver brought them back to her. At first she offered him five hundred marks reward, but then increased it to eight hundred. The incident got into the German press as an example of meanness, as the law apparently required a ten per cent reward and the sour comment was made that in Russia Pavlova would never have got her jewels back at all! In eastern markets, Pavlova sometimes haggled over absurdly small amounts or paid equally absurd large ones for trifles.

Her generosity did not stem simply from a lack of appreciation of the value of money, though sometimes that contributed to it. It stemmed from a warm and sincere feeling for people. When she met people she radiated interest in them, perhaps in rather a naive way; Muriel Stuart compared her to Billy Graham in the way she spread happiness and uplift. She took the trouble to talk to the lonely old women who waited for her at stage doors, just as much as to dance teachers and fond parents of would-be ballerinas. Young girls embraced by her remembered it forever: Agnes de Mille threw herself on the ground, prayed God to make her worthy, and kept the flowers Pavlova had given her for ten years. She said Pavlova was an apostle who had the power of conversion. Raymond Marriott, a British theatre journalist, told me how impressed he was when, as a teen-age boy in Manchester, he asked to interview Pavlova for the local paper. He accompanied her on a tour of the work rooms of a dress shop and was astonished by the way she spent about an hour talking to the girls and asking about their work.

Pavlova gave the impression of being genuinely interested in the girls; they liked her enormously, and cheered when she left. Marriott went back to Pavlova's hotel for tea. 'Pavlova was, I think, looking back, a bit amused by me being so young—I was still in short trousers. I remember how much at home she made me feel and that she asked me a lot of questions about what I did, what I wanted to do, and so forth. This could not have been for publicity, for she knew I was a youth of no importance whatsoever. In addition to her loveliness, her charm and grace were enchanting, unforgettable, and one really did feel a thrill from her simple, unaffected kindliness'.

Some people found Pavlova's conversation too unsophisticated or her manner, when being amusing, too arch. Alexandre Benois, for example, compared her unfavourably in this respect with Karsavina. 'Unlike Pavlova, with whom one could not talk except in a half-coquettish ballet fashion, Karsavina was capable of sustaining a serious conversation.'

But most people surrendered to Pavlova's charm, humour, vivacity and simple elegance. Although she was most at home speaking Russian or French, she spoke a fluent but idiosyncratic broken English. (Some authors have attempted to reproduce her style of speech when quoting her words: I have transcribed them into normal English, just as the articles published in her name were invariably edited and re-written for her.) In Hollywood, she was very friendly with Mary Pickford, Douglas Fairbanks and Charles Chaplin; at Ivy House she regularly entertained numerous theatrical and artistic personalities. According to Sol Hurok she was full of life, gesticulating a great deal, laughing a lot in a rich, hearty way, and never wearing 'the mask of a ballerina'. When she was interviewed by the *Sydney Morning Herald* in 1926, the reporter described her in similar terms. He said she resembled the singer Galli-Curci in appearance and talked with charming vivacity, with pretty playing of the hands and shrugging of the shoulders. But she adopted a sedate air, a stately gravity, when she spoke of her art.

This contrast between the serious ballerina and the frivolous, child-like private-life personality has often been noted. She loved being 'naughty', doing things of which Dandré disapproved, when he was away or not looking. For example, she was a very bad swimmer and he objected to her taking the risk, so she loved jumping into a pool when he was not around. Hurok said she also enjoyed fun-fairs, giggling in the distorting mirrors, and she liked night-clubs and gambling. After dinner it was always, 'Well, what should we do now?'

Hurok, Pavlova and some others once went to a fairly risqué cabaret in Montmartre. Dandré was not with them, and Pavlova was like a young girl who had escaped from her chaperone. Hurok suggested that Pavlova should wear a veil, but she said: 'What if someone does see me? I am not going to hide behind my veil! And besides, how can I drink champagne through a veil?' On another occasion, when they went to hear Florence Mills at a night-club in New York, stink bombs were thrown as a demonstration by members of the staff who were on strike. Pavlova refused to leave, saying to the protesting Hurok: 'What's the matter? Must you have only perfume around you?' In Japan, Olivéroff and a dancer called Michael Nicholoff were invited by Pavlova to go on a secret rickshaw ride with her to a geisha house. Pavlova was as excited as a small child over the expedition, clenching her hand and pressing it to her mouth. She loved the house, the garden and the geishas' clothes, and she drank a lot of saké and cognac. Olivéroff says this was the occasion when she first got the idea of doing an oriental ballet, which eventually became *Oriental Impressions*.

A similar expedition took place in Shanghai when Pavlova went with Olivéroff and Nicholoff to a roadhouse which had balalaika music and Russian caviare. But Pavlova was recognized by some of the Russian émigrés in the restaurant, people started staring at her, and the band struck up the Tsarist anthem. Pavlova naturally had to stand and acknowledge an ovation but her evening 'away from it all' was spoiled. She asked the Chinese proprietress of the restaurant to recommend a typical local night-club where she could go unrecognized. The woman arranged for Pavlova and her party to go to a cabaret in the native quarter, and she gave Pavlova an amber bead necklace as a kind of admission pass. The cabaret turned out to be intimate and 'dubious' with lots of girls in extravagant costumes, and the outing was a great success. Pavlova kept the bead necklace as a souvenir and as a lucky mascot.

Pavlova's moods changed quickly from excited delight to silent depression. Sometimes she would sit in silence, oblivious of everything around her, biting her knuckles or sucking one of the bits of amber in her 'Shanghai' necklace. Sometimes she would cry. Never were her quick changes of mood and temper more obvious than when she played poker. She looked glum when she had a bad hand and would be very depressed when she lost, telling Dandré to pay up for her. She tried, not very successfully, to look indifferent when she had a good hand and when she won she announced gleefully that it would be all her own money. She was like a child at play.

She was always smartly but simply dressed and made up. Her jewellery was usually limited to a plain pearl necklace; she kept her diamonds and other jewellery in the bank. She used very little facial make-up off stage: no skin creams or lotions, just plain white vaseline. Her perfume was usually a light lily of the valley cologne, an aroma which she particularly liked. She wore tailored suits by day and classical gowns by night; her dresses were simple, soft and clinging, and she never wore corsets. She was conservative about clothes, often ordering copies of dresses which she already possessed. Even cheap ready-made clothes looked elegant on her. Her shopping expeditions for clothes were a bit like a child's; she played with the model gowns in the fashion-houses, changing them around so much that she was virtually designing her own clothes. She did the same thing with fancy hats. Her main difficulty was in buying shoes; just as with her ballet shoes, she was always discarding street shoes as being too tight or in some other way uncomfortable. She constantly bought new ones, and usually travelled with about three dozen pairs. Her friends dreaded an invitation to go out buying shoes with her, as it would inevitably be a long and difficult expedition.

All Pavlova's shopping was erratic; C. W. Beaumont told me how she used to come into his bookshop, have half the things on the shelves taken down and shown to her, and then leave without buying anything. Walford Hyden recounted an early morning visit to Covent Garden market when some flowers Pavlova bought became mislaid. The salesman offered her some others but she was indignant: 'Where are *my* flowers? Why do you think I come here so early in the morning if it is to be given the second-best?' When the salesman confessed that her flowers had been sent in a van to Oxford by mistake, Pavlova insisted on being driven after the van, catching it up at Reading and returning to Ivy House by breakfast time with the flowers she had originally chosen!

Fastidiousness about clothes, books and flowers was extended to everything around her. Pavlova liked everything to be 'just so', and to satisfy her sense of form. On one of her last European tours Dr Julian Braunsweg, the impresario, found her moving a heavy wardrobe around her hotel bedroom. She did not like the 'line' it made where it stood and was moving it to a more 'artistic' position.

Not only was Pavlova often child-like in her moods and in her behaviour; she was also instinctively good with children and regretted not having any of her own. She apparently had some physical abnormality which would have required an operation to make child-bearing possible. There is a story that a doctor in Russia told her that God had made her for a greater purpose than having children; Mme Manya said Pavlova was afraid that the operation might affect her dancing. In later years Pavlova was conscious of

what she had missed. She sometimes said that the greatest
mistake of her life was not having a child or she would ask
a friend if she should give up dancing to have a child, as
though seeking reassurance that she had made the right
choice. Rita Glynde told me that Pavlova once found her
making a white brassière on a train. Brassières in those days
were colloquially known as 'BBs', or 'bust bodices'. When
Pavlova asked Miss Glynde what she was doing, the flus-
tered fifteen-year-old girl answered, 'I'm making a BB',
pronouncing the initials in a way which sounded to Pavlova
like 'bébé'. Pavlova, looking astonished, asked 'You are
having a baby?' and when Miss Glynde had explained,
Pavlova confessed 'I would like a baby'. Pavlova once fondled
two naked babies in a street in India, and cried when she had
to leave them, which Walford Hyden took as a sign of
thwarted mother love.

Apart from any physical difficulty, Pavlova shared the
natural fear of every ballerina that child-bearing might
affect her career. Some dancers have successfully returned
to the stage after having children, even after having twins,
though I do not think any of the world's greatest ballerinas
have done so. Neither the enforced absence from the stage
and from class, nor the emotional separation from the
theatre, is easily reconciled with the demands made on a
star dancer. Pavlova was emphatic that experience of love
was essential in a dancer's emotional development; she was
equally emphatic that the experience must be transmuted
into artistry, and not allowed to dominate a dancer's life.
This is how she explained it to Olivéroff:

'To be a great artist, you must have loved, you must know
all about love . . . you must suffer with love. But—listen to
me, *galoupshik* (silly boy)—you must learn to do *without* it!
You must dance your love, you must spiritualize it, you
must turn it into grace and beauty of movement and line—
you must turn it into a living flame upon the stage, so that
you will kindle your audiences and lift them with you into
the sacred fire. In the end, that is the only way for any artist

to love, who would be great. And that is the only love that endures, the only love that never changes!'

There were some girls in the company who were 'afraid of love' and this is what Pavlova said about them: 'I have trained them beautifully—you see how they can dance. But what does their dancing mean, after all? What does it make you feel? You do not feel like shouting, or like weeping—or like getting on your knees! No, they do not give you any emotion when they dance, they do not move you. And why? Well, one reason is, that they will not have lovers. They cannot bring themselves to love, not really love. They will not love until they get married—and then it will be too late for their dancing.'

Many members of Pavlova's company found it impossible to believe that she ever had love affairs. She certainly did, sometimes with dancers in the company. But in accordance with her sense of propriety and what was fitting, these affairs were conducted so discreetly that scarcely anybody knew about them. Mordkin's widow told me that Pavlova used to confide some of the details to her, and other dancers have told me of their various suspicions.

Pavlova was susceptible to sheer physical attraction. She once pointed out a stage hand to Olivéroff and said: 'That is my idea of a man! That man would make for me a wonderful lover.' But when Olivéroff asked her 'Why not?', she said 'Ah no . . . for me that must always be a long story.' She was excited by the men in Japan, and frequently remarked on their physical beauty, adding significantly that they would probably make very faithful lovers. For what she was seeking, especially in later life, was companionship and understanding.

She did not very much enjoy sex as such, and she certainly did not approve of casual promiscuity. On one occasion in Egypt, she had been asked to present a signed photograph of herself as a prize to the best contestant at a costume ball in Alexandria. She was horrified when the award went to a notorious courtesan and pretended that she had no photo available. She told Theodore Stier afterwards that the idea of her photo in such a woman's boudoir was utterly intolerable. Prince Koschubei used to tell his friends in Paris that Pavlova had been a frigid lover. She herself once said that sex had to be taken like medicine—'it is nasty at first but it does you good.' I have been told that she was actually afraid of normal intercourse, fearing it might do her physical damage, and that she preferred some form of oral sex. And towards the end of her career she got much of her friendship and companionship from the attractive young American homosexuals she recruited for her company. These were not always very good dancers—one former member of the company told me 'they were better at making fancy costumes out of beads and things than at dancing, but they looked very decorative on the stage'—though some of them *were* good dancers and took leading parts. Pavlova loved going out to night-clubs and cabarets with them, hearing about their loves and adventures and even asking them for intimate physical details of what they did. They were good company and they 'flirted' with Pavlova in what would now be called a 'camp' way, which appealed to the coquettish side of her nature.

People who do not themselves find very much satisfaction in a normal sexual relationship sometimes compensate for this by being very flirtatious and coquettish, either in real life or on the stage, or both. A person may be extremely convincing in a seductive role on the stage yet quite frigid in a real-life sexual encounter. This may be one motive for taking up a stage career. It has frequently been noted that actors often complain that they do not have a clear sense of their own identities; they feel more like real people when they are adopting someone else's identity than they do when trying to be themselves in everyday life.

This may well have been true of Pavlova, and indeed everything about her personality and behaviour fits into a fairly well-established psychological pattern. Children who are brought up by only one parent, and without much contact with other children, commonly find it difficult to establish satisfactory personal relationships and to become mature adults. Because of their early isolation and lack of easy and natural contact with children of the opposite sex, the opposite sex tends to remain a mystery. A girl with no father or brothers may tend to romanticize boys as heroes, or caricature them as monsters, and this distortion may remain in adult life. Just as in childhood lonely children of this kind find alternatives to normal play with other children, so in adult life they find alternatives to normal intimate relationships.

The young Pavlova, a delicate only child, spent her time reading, sewing and communing with nature. Even at ballet school she was segregated from boys and from the outside world. An isolated childhood of this kind can easily lead to an unusually close communion with animals, as it did for Beatrix Potter. People brought up in this way often remain 'loners', better at managing themselves and other people than at co-operating in a team. They are afraid of getting too closely involved, physically or psychologically, with anyone else. Their isolation, aloofness and apparent non-sexuality make them seem very different from the common run of humanity, so that they are often condemned as inhuman or admired as superhuman.

Pavlova's strong ambition to be a great ballerina may well have been the result of a desire to overcome the disadvantages of illegitimate birth and of childhood poverty. Her enthusiasm and empathy for the more sentimental and romantic types of ballet were probably a symptom of sexual non-fulfilment. Even her adversity in times of illness and pain, and her ability to carry on touring and dancing in hard conditions, are to some extent typical of this type of personality. People who do not greatly depend on sensual, physical pleasures do not so much mind bodily discomforts.

So there is nothing really surprising in Pavlova's complex personality: her childishness, her naiveté, her aura of spirituality, her volatile changing of moods, her skill as an actress and her dedicated hard work as a dancer. It is not surprising either that members of her company rarely felt that they understood her, that her relationships with everyone, including Dandré, fell short of complete intimacy, and that she was virtually worshipped by many dancers and by audiences all over the world. She remained a lonely child, without close friends and without real husband or family. (Her mother came to England for three weeks in 1924, stayed at Ivy House, saw Pavlova dance in Bournemouth, and then returned to Russia. Pavlova was delighted to see her but by this time they had very little in common.) She was a child with the luck and the skill—the genius perhaps —to have found an adult calling in which she was supreme. Her dancing brought her as near happiness as she could ever be and her life would have been empty without it. That is why her early death, before age forced her to retire from the stage, was not such a tragedy as it might seem.

CHAPTER EIGHT

Immortal Swan

CHANGES in Pavlova herself, as well as in her repertoire, were noted by various people in the years before her death. In the last months it almost seemed as if she had a premonition of the end. Naturally, as she approached fifty, she was less inclined and less able to do her most energetic and fast-moving dances; she suffered increasingly from her knee injury and during her early forties she put on weight though in her final years she again became extremely thin. *Les Papillons* was not in the repertoire after about 1919 and *The Dragonfly* and *Valse Caprice* were rarely if ever performed in her final tours. Opinions differ about how well Pavlova continued to dance the items which did remain in her repertoire. Marie-Thérèse Duncan told me that by 1927 Pavlova was very sad to watch, and appeared to have lost the joy in her dancing. Serge Lifar, who saw her in her final season at Golders Green in 1930, said her arabesques were still sublime and she still palpitated with divine energy, but she got little applause. Afterwards he asked her why she still gave so many performances, 'in which so little of the real thing is left'. But she gave no indication of giving up; she said she had to go on spreading beauty among the people, and apparently she even discussed the possibility of dancing with Lifar in the future. Algeranoff said that she still looked incredibly young as Lise in *La Fille Mal Gardée*, younger than the girls in the corps who were actually thirty years junior to her. I suspect that, as with all ballerinas who continue dancing towards the age of fifty, her performances became much more variable. This would account for the very different impressions recorded by various reliable observers.

Clearly those who remembered the Pavlova of former years were aware of something missing; equally clearly, she could still use her personality and her remaining technique to exercise a powerful theatrical magic. Unfortunately, time was passing in more senses than one. Audiences were beginning to find her productions too old-fashioned; her company was not in such demand as before, and it had to be reduced in size. For the final European tours, in 1930 and 1931, many of the older and more experienced dancers were dispensed with, on the grounds that if anyone had to go they were the ones who could most easily find other engagements. The result was that the company was younger and contained fewer strong personalities than usual. Dr Julian Braunsweg, who was associated with the promotion of the 1930 tour, thought that the company was poor and that Pavlova's technique was going. But he still found himself drawn, night after night, to watch the part of the programme in which she danced, and he still surrendered to her magnetic personality.

Mme Borovansky said that in those last years Pavlova allowed herself to look untidy and bedraggled in rehearsals, and used quite frequently to say 'I'm getting old'. But, in Mme Borovansky's opinion, Pavlova nearly always succeeded in transforming herself into her usual elegant, young-looking personality on the stage. Like Algeranoff, she noted that Pavlova had nothing to fear in looks or personality from the younger girls of the corps. If Pavlova got slacker about her own off-stage appearance, she also to some extent relaxed her strictness with the company. Mary Skeaping once tripped over another dancer's dress during a performance and fell flat. Pavlova, who in the past would have been furious, simply laughed and the whole company burst into laughter. Eventually Pavlova simply said 'That's enough; joke over.'

When Pavlova's energy flagged, or she was occasionally tempted to take a long holiday instead of doing another tour, it was Dandré who egged her on and pressed ahead with arrangements for more appearances. Some people think he was motivated by greed and they accuse him of helping to kill Pavlova with over-work. In his book *The Three Graces*, Serge Lifar told an unkind story of Dandré, immediately after Pavlova's death, saying 'What a ruinous loss—what an amount of business gone west!' But, as we have already noted, Pavlova herself had an immense inner compulsion to dance. She also had a great revulsion at the idea of living on beyond the time when she could dance. Walford Hyden recalled her saying: 'I shall die before any of you; I do not think I could possibly grow old and die slowly.'

Had she lived, it is of course possible that Pavlova would have found a way of growing old without having to 'die slowly'. Most dancers feel that the end of their dancing careers is bound to be the end of their lives; but in fact many of them find new careers, perhaps in marriage and family life, perhaps in producing or choreographing ballets, perhaps in teaching. Pavlova might have developed her talents as a choreographer; she had already told Walford Hyden that she was planning to make a ballet to an orchestral version of Bach's well-known Toccata and Fugue. Or she might have continued to run a company, without herself dancing in it, and she might even have played a crucial direct role in the development of British ballet, which was just about to be born when she died. But she did not look forward to any non-dancing future, and it was not to be.

After her final British tour, which ended at Golders Green on December 13th 1930, Pavlova went to Cannes in the south of France to rest and relax. Felia Doubrovska recalled the New Year's Eve dinner party in Cannes at the end of 1930, just a month before Pavlova's death. Everyone in the restaurant applauded her when she came in, but she was sad and in poor humour. A window was open and a pigeon landed on her shoulder, which disquieted her. (There was a Russian superstition that a bird flying into a room was an omen of death, and this followed the omen of the wreath at Golders Green.) Five minutes after midnight, when the celebrations were just beginning, Pavlova led her party home to her hotel. She sent them all to bed but she did not go to bed herself. Instead she sat up talking with Pianowski, her ballet-master, and then visited the flower-market early in the morning and took flowers to the grave of the Russian Grand Duke Nicholas in the Cannes ceme-tery. At nine in the morning, Pavlova was back in her hotel, having left her room unoccupied all night, and she began to get ready for the day's engagements. Doubrovska received an early morning bouquet of flowers delivered with greet-ings from Pavlova by the hotel porter.

Maybe Pavlova really had a presentiment of death; maybe some of her friends merely read this into her actions after the event. Certainly she was not suffering from any illness, other than a possible wearying of the spirit. Her death was the result of an accident. The night train on which Pavlova was travelling from Cannes to Paris collided with a goods train and Pavlova got out to see what was happening. This had no apparent effect on her health, but it seems likely that she caught a chill. In Paris, practising in Leo Staats' studio, she complained of cold and began to cough. She was rehearsing with a temperature and one night she collapsed in her bedroom. She had to be supported to the train taking her to The Hague, where her 1931 tour was due to begin. Pavlova's personal physician in Paris, Dr Zalewsky, thought she was not well enough to travel.

As soon as she arrived in The Hague, on Saturday, January 17th, she went straight to bed at the Hotel des Indes and the local doctor diagnosed pleurisy in the left lung. The next day a second doctor confirmed this diagnosis and pres-cribed alcohol, which Pavlova refused to take. She would not even take a tot of rum in her tea. According to Dandré, she still intended to dance, as scheduled, on the next day, but by then she had difficulty in breathing and could only take small sips of warm milk. By Tuesday, the doctors were becoming seriously worried and on Wednesday Dr Zalewsky arrived from Paris.

Dandré said that on Wednesday Pavlova was still talking business and discussing the repertoire and arrangements for rehearsals. According to him she seemed very clear in her mind and did not realize the seriousness of her condition. On the other hand Nina Kirsanova remembered Pavlova telling her the end was near and asking her to go and pray in a Russian Orthodox Church. By Thursday, the inflammation had spread to the right lung, she was given a serum injection and her back was pierced to remove fluid. In the evening she lost consciousness and began to breathe faster and faster. At midnight she opened her eyes, tried to cross herself and whispered to her maid: 'Get my *Swan* costume ready.' Half an hour later, she was dead. Dandré, Dr Zalewsky and her maid were present in the room. It was Friday, January 23rd, just a week before her fiftieth birthday.

Pavlova's body was dressed in her favourite beige lace dress and she was covered with her beloved lilac sprigs. A Russian Orthodox mass for the dead was said before her body was transferred to the chapel of a Roman Catholic monastery, and then to St Philip's Russian Orthodox Church in London, where her body lay in state for a day and a half. Crowds of people thronged the church, even insisting on admission after it was closed; their tributes ranged from expensive wreaths to humble posies. Black-edged memorial cards were on sale outside the church. The church was packed for the funeral service on Thursday, January 29th. Then the cortège stopped for a short time outside Ivy House before proceeding to Golders Green crematorium, where a Russian choir sang. Sablin, a White Russian diplomat, lent the Imperial flag to be draped over the coffin till the last moment. Later, at a memorial service in New York, the distinguished modern dancer Ruth St Denis said: 'Pavlova lived on the threshold of heaven and earth as an interpreter of the ways of God.'

Pavlova's securities in the United States had been managed

for her by Otto Kahn, the impresario who first invited her to the Metropolitan Opera House, and she left about $377,000. In London, the gross value of her estate was given as just over £14,000. She left no will, and Dandré assumed he would inherit. But an action was brought to court in London in 1934 on behalf of Pavlova's aged mother, who was said to be still alive in Russia. Although Pavlova had lived in London for so many years, she had remained officially domiciled in Russia, and under Russian law her mother could claim the estate if she had been totally dependent on her daughter. Pavlova's mother never came to London to give evidence, and the case was obviously instigated by the Soviet Government which spotted a good chance to gain some foreign assets. Dandré denied that Pavlova's mother had been totally dependent on her though they had always given the old lady an allowance. He claimed that he and Pavlova were legally married in 1914; Sol Hurok signed a document testifying to the essential part played by Dandré in managing Pavlova's company and in making her success possible. Nevertheless Pavlova's mother (or the Soviet Government) succeeded in winning the case and most of Pavlova's British assets went to Russia.

Ivy House and its contents were sold by auction; at first the house was used as a hospital but later it again became an artistic centre. At the time of writing it is a municipal college of speech and drama, but the 'swan lake' is empty and there are prefabricated huts in the garden for the students. A blue plaque at the entrance, provided by Hendon Corporation, reminds passers-by that it was Pavlova's home for nineteen years.

The contents of Ivy House are widely scattered. Some of her costumes are in the Paget-Fredericks Collection at Berkeley, University of California; others are in the London Museum. Properties used by Pavlova and statuettes of her are to be found in many private collections, and in the homes of her friends and admirers.

But plaques and other material things are no real memorial to Pavlova. A spiritual memorial is provided annually by a service in the Russian Orthodox Church in London, organized by the devoted Mme Manya. But her best memorial would have been her dancing; unfortunately neither the photographs, nor the sculptures, nor even the films, can really re-create that. In 1935 Dandré organized the making of a memorial film, *Immortal Swan*, to which I have already referred. This included several shots of her dancing and relaxing at Ivy House. The sound track had some of her favourite music, conducted by Vladimir Launitz who also arranged the score for a reconstruction of *Chopiniana* danced by former members of Pavlova's company and staged by Algeranoff and Paul Petroff. There was also a reconstruction of *Invitation to the Dance*, with Pavlova's own very graceful solo inserted, ending with her charming curtsey.

At least this film provided some sort of memento of Pavlova's dancing and personality. Dandré's attempts to preserve her company without her were doomed. (Later he managed another ballet company, which toured Australia, but this too was unsuccessful and his last years in London were spent in fairly modest circumstances, being looked after by friends. He died in 1944.) Pavlova herself had been emphatic that the company should carry on; in her last days she stressed that they must dance at a Brussels charity concert in aid of needy students. The company duly performed, the night after her death, and the music of *The Dying Swan* was played with the curtain up on an empty stage. King Albert and Queen Elizabeth of the Belgians rose and the whole audience stood throughout the music. On January 25th, the same thing was done at a performance by the Camargo Society in London. These were the first of many similar memorial performances of *The Dying Swan*, given on empty stages all over the world. Even for those who never saw Pavlova, performances like these could be moving experiences; for those who did see her, they could be unbearable.

However poignant a mental picture of this solo we may form, and however many talented dancers may attempt to recreate it, it is really only the memory of Pavlova's own performance that lives on. Yet the memory has become in some sense eternal and has exercised an enormous influence on the whole world of ballet.

Sir Frederick Ashton, the choreographer who built the greater part of the Royal Ballet's repertoire and who provided Dame Margot Fonteyn with most of her created roles, was first drawn to ballet by seeing Pavlova in Peru; her memory has inspired him ever since. Sir Robert Helpmann, who partnered Dame Margot for several years, made some memorable dramatic ballets for the Royal Ballet and then became a co-director of the Australian Ballet, was taken to see Pavlova in Australia when he was a boy, watched every performance she gave for about eight months, appeared as an extra in her production of *Don Quixote*, and was committed to ballet for life. It is impossible to count the number of girls who started learning ballet because they saw Pavlova; Tamara Toumanova was one of them. Then came a generation of girls who started learning ballet because their mothers saw Pavlova; nowadays it may be their grandmothers. I am told that Pavlova still provides one of the most popular topics for young English girls offering study projects in ballet for the General Certificate of Education. Ladies who danced with Pavlova became teachers of ballet, cherishing their memories of her methods and her standards, all over the world. Most important of all, Pavlova sowed the seed of ballet in every continent and created a world-wide audience. If Pavlova had not toured the world, giving people a new vision of beauty, ballet might never have acquired its universal appeal. It might have remained an esoteric thing, thought fit only for sophisticated aesthetes. The fact that ballet is now booming not just in capital cities, but in provincial and regional centres all over the world, is at least indirectly a tribute to Pavlova, and the best memorial she could have.

Appendix

1. THE MAIN BOOKS

Algeranoff, H.: *My Years with Pavlova* (Heinemann 1957)

Beaumont, C. W.: *Anna Pavlova* (C. W. Beaumont 1932)

Dandré, Victor: *Anna Pavlova* (Cassell 1932)

Franks, Arthur (ed.): *Pavlova* (Burke 1956)

Hyden, Walford: *Pavlova, The Genius of the Dance* (Constable 1931)

Krassovskaya, Vera: *Anna Pavlova* (USSR 1965)

— *Russian Ballet Theatre at the Beginning of the 20th Century* (USSR 1972)

Levinson, André: *La Danse d'Aujourd'hui* (Duchartre & Van Buggen-houdt, Paris 1929)

Olivéroff, André: *Flight of the Swan* (Dutton, New York 1932)

Pavlova, Anna: *Pages of My Life,* tr by Sebastien Voirol (included in *Pavlova* edited by Arthur Franks and in *Anna Pavlova* by Valerian Svetlov)

Roslavleva, Natalia: *Era of the Russian Ballet 1770–1965* (Gollancz 1966)

Stier, Theodore: *With Pavlova Around The World* (Hurst & Blackett 1929)

Svetlov, Valerian: *Terpischore* (St Petersburg 1906)

— *Anna Pavlova* (Michel de Brunoff, Paris 1922)

2. SUPPLEMENTARY BOOKS AND ARTICLES

Ballet Review (New York), Vol. 3, No. 2, 1969 (article by David Vaughan)

Beaumont, C. W.: Article in programme of Pavlova commemoration gala at Stoll Theatre, London, January 23rd 1956.

Braunsweg, Dr Julian: *Braunsweg's Ballet Scandals* (Allen & Unwin 1973)

Buckle, Richard: *Nijinsky* (Weidenfeld & Nicholson 1971)

Dance and Dancers, January 1956 (articles by Aubrey Hitchens, Sol Hurok, Mme Manya, Anna Pruzina and Mary Skeaping)

Dance Magazine (New York), August 1931 (articles by Laurent Novikoff and Hubert Stowitts)

— January 1955 (article by Nina Kirsanova)

Dancing Times, October 1934 (article by Edward J. Kurylo)

— August 1964 (article by Tamara Karsavina)

— October 1971 & March 1972 (articles by Nesta Macdonald)

de Mille, Agnes: *Dance to the Piper* (Hamish Hamilton, 1951)

Fokine, Michel: *Memoirs of a Ballet Master* (Constable 1961)

Graves, Dr A. Karl: *How I Became A Secret Agent* (included in *Fifty Amazing Secret Service Dramas* (Odhams))

Haskell, Arnold: Introduction to catalogue of Pavlova exhibition, London Museum 1956

Hurok, Sol: *Impresario* (Macdonald 1947)
Karsavina, Tamara: *Theatre Street* (Heinemann 1930)
Lifar, Serge: *Diaghilev* (Putnam 1940)
— *The Three Graces* (Cassell 1959)
Lilly, Doris: *Those Fabulous Greeks* (Cowles, New York 1970; W. H. Allen, London 1971)
Oukrainsky, Serge: *My Years with Pavlova* (Suttonhouse, USA 1940)
Strand Magazine, Oct. 1913 & Dec. 1926 (articles by Pavlova)
— Oct. 1924 (article by Sidney Dark)

3. DANCERS AND COLLEAGUES OF PAVLOVA'S WHOM I CONSULTED

Pauline Barton, Xenia Borovansky, Hilda Butsova, Manya Charchev-nikova, Kathleen Crofton, Felia Doubrovska, Winifred Edwards, Rozella Frey, Rita Glynde, Anna Ivanova, Juliet Jarvis, Mme Mordkin, Cléo Nordi, Ruth Page, Mary Skeaping, Muriel Stuart, Joan van Wart, Dr Julian Braunsweg, Edward Caton, Maestro Celli, Sir Robert Help-mann, Sol Hurok, Leon Kellaway, Harry Mills, and Alexandre Tcherepnine.

4. OTHERS WHO HELPED WITH INFORMATION OR ADVICE

IN BRITAIN: Sir Frederick Ashton, Robert Baker, Cyril W. Beaumont, Alan Blyth, Jeremy Bolton (of the British Film Institute), Richard Bonynge, Mary Clarke (Editor of the *Dancing Times*), David Leonard and John O'Brien (of the Ballet Bookshop), Nesta Macdonald, Raymond Marriott, Nadia Nerina, Mr and Mrs John Percival, Alexander Poliakoff, Dame Marie Rambert, Vera Russell, Boris Skidelsky (of the Royal Opera House, Covent Garden), Dr Anthony Storr, Peter Williams (Editor of *Dance and Dancers*), G. B. L. Wilson, Marc M. Wolff.
IN THE UNITED STATES: Jack Anderson, Mr and Mrs Clive Barnes, George Dorris, Marie-Thérèse Duncan, Madeleine Gutman, Russell Hartley, Victoria Huckenpahler, Anatol Joukowsky, Zelda Mortimer, Renèe Renouf, Francis Robinson (of the Metropolitan Opera House), Anatol Vilzak and Genevieve Oswald and her staff at the Dance Col-lection of the Library and Museum of Performing Arts, New York.
IN ARGENTINA: Theo Peters and Reg Praeger of the British Embassy, Angel Fumagalli and Luis Angel Torres.
IN AUSTRALIA: Edward H. Pask and Noel Pelly of the Australian Ballet.
IN AUSTRIA: Alfred Oberzaucher.
IN DENMARK: Susanne Lund of the Royal Danish Ballet.
IN FINLAND: Kiril Grigorkoff, Margareta Grigorkoff.
IN GERMANY: Klaus Geitel, Horst Koegler.
IN THE NETHERLANDS: Joel Kasow, Leon Koning.

Index

About the Author

OLEG KERENSKY was born in London in 1930 of Russian parents. His grandfather, Alexander Feodorovich Kerensky, was head of the Russian Provisional Government in 1917. His father is a leading British designer of bridges and motorways.

Educated at Westminster School and Christ Church, Oxford, he was Treasurer and Librarian of the Oxford Union. He worked in the BBC for fifteen years, for the last five of these as deputy editor of the *Listener*. He is now a free-lance journalist and broadcaster, specializing in the arts.

Besides being ballet critic of the *Daily Mail* and *New Statesman*, Oleg Kerensky is an occasional contributor to *The Times*, the *Guardian*, and the *Dancing Times*. He has broadcast in *The Critics, The Lively Arts, The World of Books, The Arts This Week, Ten O'Clock* and in the BBC's European and World Services and has also appeared in *Release* on BBC2.